I0643911

Pagan Portals

Sage Advice

A Practical Guide to Energetic Smoke Cleansing and House Blessing

What People Are Saying About

Sage Advice

I have had the pleasure of working with Dawn Leith Dougherty of Tree of Life Incenses for several years, and her smudge blends are nothing short of extraordinary. Dawn's extensive knowledge of herbs and her intuitive abilities make her blends uniquely beneficial. Her ability to create blends that resonate on a deep, energetic level sets her apart from others in the field. People benefit immensely from Dawn's smoke-cleansing knowledge because she understands the properties of each herb and how they interact with each other. Her intuitive approach ensures that every blend is not only aromatic but also energetically potent. Dawn's Tree of Life Incenses have been an integral part of my spell kits, providing the perfect complement to my own creations. I wholeheartedly endorse Dawn Dougherty and Tree of Life Incenses for anyone seeking superior smudge blends and incense mixes that truly make a difference in their spiritual practice.
Loren Morris, Primitive Witchery, author of *Braiding Magic: The Art of Crafting Witches Spell Cords*

Dawn Leith Dougherty carries extensive knowledge surrounding incense herbs and the intentions for what they are used for within the practice of smudging. Her book is practical, easy to read, and makes a wonderful addition to any bookshelf. I use each and every blend that she makes during my spiritual practices and healing work, and can attest not only to the effectiveness but also to the delicious lingering aroma that the blends leave behind. I highly endorse *Sage Advice*!
Lynn Green, healer, medium & co-host of *Ohm-g Podcast*

Pagan Portals

Sage Advice

A Practical Guide to Energetic Smoke Cleansing and House Blessing

Dawn Leith Dougherty

MOON BOOKS
London, UK
Washington, DC, USA

CollectiveInk

First published by Moon Books, 2025
Moon Books is an imprint of Collective Ink Ltd.,
Unit 11, Shepperton House, 89 Shepperton Road, London, N1 3DF
office@collectiveinkbooks.com
www.collectiveinkbooks.com
www.moon-books.net

For distributor details and how to order please visit the 'Ordering' section on our website.

ISBN: 978 1 80341 940 4
978 1 80341 939 8 (ebook)
Library of Congress Control Number: 2024945621

A CIP catalogue record for this book is available from the British Library.

Design: Lapiz Digital Services

UK: Printed and bound by CPI Group (UK) Ltd, Croydon, CR0 4YY
US: Printed and bound by Thomson-Shore, 7300 West Joy Road, Dexter, MI 48130

Contents

Disclaimer

It must be stated here that the information provided in this book is solely for entertainment purposes. I do not guarantee the accuracy of the information contained herein, and some is considered to be the opinion of Dawn Leith Dougherty. All details contained in these pages can in no way diagnose or treat ailments or disease, or be taken as medical or health advice. Please consult a qualified medical practitioner for advice pertaining to your health issues. Dawn Leith Dougherty will not accept responsibility or liability whatsoever for injury, loss, or damage incurred by you, the reader, as a direct or indirect result of the guidance shared here. Recommendations and links contained herein and any information or products gleaned from them are to be considered for entertainment purposes. Any purchases made by you or websites visited as a direct or indirect result of reading this book are done at your own risk. By reading this book, you accept this disclaimer. It is recommended to do your own research on topics of interest to you.

Dawn Leith Dougherty

Preface

Smoke cleansing and house blessing should be fairly simple, fun, and straightforward. If you have been a bit frustrated trying to wade through complicated rituals or information pertaining to a culture or spiritual path to which you feel you may not belong or do not resonate with, never fear, help is here! While I use the word "smudging" often in this book for purposes of clarity, know that I am referring to "smoke cleansing" as a regular practice which can be done by anyone, as opposed to "Smudging Ceremony," which is an indigenous Native American ceremonial closed practice. Much information is readily available in other books and on the internet, however, my intent is to put some of the basics and background information together in one place, and weed out what may not be necessary for general practice. Many times in my business I am asked a full gamut of questions about this topic, so decided to write about it, with many of my answers and advice to my customers edited into book form. Also included here is my own knowledge base from working with energetic herbs and resins, trials and errors, my own personal ritual and intentions, and dos and don'ts. My information and knowledge over the years come from my own research, personal experiences, and my own unverified personal gnosis (UPG). This book will address practical, simple, and everyday smoke cleansing practices to which folk of all ages, spiritual paths, religions, and cultures can identify and adopt. You will learn the reasons for energetic smudging and have a greater understanding of how this practice affects your home and personal space in a positive manner. You will learn all you need to know about how to make this an easy and rewarding part of your journey on this beautiful planet we call home.

I hope you enjoy this book and learn from it. I am honored to share information with you which I have learned over the years, that has contributed to my own daily health and wellness practices, as well as my spiritual path. May this book be an important part of your smoke cleansing practices.

Gratitude and blessings, Dawn Leith Dougherty

Introduction

> *The word 'smudge' comes from the old English word smogen. It is cited in several dictionaries as coming from 1400–50 late Middle English. It means to smear, blur, obscure, to smother with smoke, to use dense smoke to protect an area from insects. Another meaning is also 'taken by surprise'. In English the term 'smudge' also means smut or dirt. It has been in use since the 15th century, and first appeared after the Norman conquest, so it's certainly of Germanic origin.*
>
> – Rachel Patterson[1]

Burning herbs and resins for many purposes is a tradition as old as time, utilized by peoples of many spiritual and religious traditions. Many plants have individual healing properties, known to our ancient ancestors, and used and appreciated in modern times, as well.

Indigenous peoples of the Americas, as well as those following a Western New Age spiritual path will sometimes use the term "smoke bowl blessing" for this practice, which is an important clearing and cleansing technique for your body, hearth, and home. Smudging is a recommended and welcome practice on a frequent basis to clear low or stagnant energy, clear your body and mind after a hard day's work, and to purify the air during and after illnesses of all kinds. It is also a wonderful way to cleanse new items entering your home, or after visitors exit, to neutralize and clear the air. Smoke cleansing can, and should, be done before and after ritual of any tradition, to create or clear sacred space, and charge ritual tools.

Many of you are new to smoke cleansing, or may have seen it done at some point, but wondered what it was all about. Some of you may know about white sage bundles, but are unaware of or unfamiliar with other plants and resins that can be added to your incense and cleansing practices. There are a myriad of herbs, weeds, flowers, and tree resins that have physical, mental, as well as energetic healing properties, and can be added to your smoke bowl, some of which can be easily obtained, grown, or wild harvested by you. I will address some of the more common ones in this book.

In this book you will find some easy rituals and suggestions to enhance your own lifestyle. You may find that you will be able to add to and deepen spiritual practices in ways of your own choosing, or even strip it down to basics, "woo" it up or dial it down, it all works in the way you intend. What you will not find in this book is advocation of or denigration of any specific culture or spiritual path. All are free to walk their own paths, know that energetic smudging practices are non-denominational, and transcend any religious beliefs held by myself or anyone reading this book. My experiences align with many others' and reflect what I have written in this book. I encourage you to create your own experiences, blends, and notes about how incense, herbs, and resins work for you, because everyone experiences things in their own individual way. Smudging/smoke cleansing is an ancient and respected practice done by many cultures of the world, and pre-dates any modern spiritual dogmas.

Chapter 1

Smudging Practices of the Ancients

Light the incense! You have to burn to be fragrant
~ Rumi

In ancient times, indigenous peoples of the world worked with the plant kingdom and elementals of nature. Our ancestors considered the "plant people" as intelligent and respected beings, as they did the animal kingdom. They knew what plants and their roots, stems, fruits, flowers, and leaves were to be used for food and medicine, how to prepare them, and which ones to avoid. They believed that their gods provided these sacred beings to them for the purposes of food and medicine, and used them, as well as harvested them, with great respect. Ancient peoples not only lived on the earth, but with the earth and her cycles and seasons. They were aware and watchful of plant and animal behavior, and learned which plants were healing or harmful by watching wildlife, as well as their own trial and error. They touched, tasted, and smelled most everything, and intuited energetic properties of natural materials by using them in their own daily lives and ceremonies.

Humans in past times knew these things and used plant resins (like frankincense, myrrh, copal etc.), woods such as sandalwood, palo santo, and agarwood, as well as herbs like rosemary, lavender, cedar, and sages to keep illness away and to cleanse their space, and in sacred rituals. Incense (which in Latin means "to arouse" in regard to emotions) of various kinds has been used in all ancient cultures. Unlike today, where some people burn incense sticks as a room freshener, incenses were burned to honor their deities, banish insects, demons and evil spirits, purify and consecrate the air in ceremonies and in temples, and burned in hospitals, sickrooms, and funerals to kill bacteria and viruses and keep illness away (as well as noxious smells), which was one of the original uses for frankincense and myrrh. Obviously, people didn't know microbes existed then, but knew their herbs and resins could potentially keep sickness that led to disease at bay. Hippocrates was known to have helped drive away plague by having the city of Athens burn herbs throughout the entire city. Sacred smoke is considered to be an herbal messenger to the gods, like a bridge from earth to the heavens. A stone tablet from around 1500 B.C.E. at the Sphinx in Egypt describes these practices. Spices, herbs, and resins were highly prized by these ancient peoples, so much so that some of them were considered to be gifts worthy only of their kings and queens, or the ruling classes. Wise people and medicine folk used (and still do) smoke from incense in their divination practices, as well as prescribe it for natural healing of ailments. As an energy practitioner, I cleanse myself and my tools before any work that I am doing, no matter what.

Western peoples may be somewhat familiar with the Native American smudging practices, many of which include cedar, sweetgrass, and white sage, and have probably seen white sage smudge sticks, and these are now fairly commonly shared worldwide. There are numerous tribes throughout the Americas, so the herbs and methods used can differ from region to region. The sacred smoke bowl blessing is one term for the clearing of space, honoring of spirit, and the beginning of ceremony in many Native American traditions. The five elements are represented in incense ceremonies from many cultures which include earth, air, fire, water, and the smoke is ether or spirit. The vessel used differs also from tribe to tribe, as some use abalone or other shells for the water element, and others do not, believing the water element negates the fire element. Birds and their feathers are highly revered, and represent the element of air. Feathers, feather wands, and wings are used by peoples all over the world to disperse smoke and in brushing away unwanted energy. Tobacco is also sacred to the North American indigenous people, and used in pipe ceremonies, as offering to nature spirits, as well as Great Spirit. Sacred herbal smoke carries intentions, prayers, and wishes to the realms of the gods and ancestors.

In Central American cultures, the tree resin, copal, is frequently used, and is also one of my personal favorites. Copal can inspire insights, a way to see subtle energy, and in *Popol Vuh,* ("Book of Community") the K'iche peoples' story of creation, it is described as a "seeing instrument." Amazon cultures revere the beautiful and sweet palo santo or "Holy Wood." Palo Santo is a protected tree and should be sustainably harvested. Only fallen wood is harvested, and then only if the wood has been aged for at least four to ten years. Only then can it be used, and the fragrant oils in the wood are more concentrated.

European people would burn sages, mugwort, and other herbs that grow there, as well as oak moss, and evergreens such as pine and cedar. The practice of saining, comes from Scottish folk magic fumigation practices meant to purify, heal, protect, and bless. People would burn pine bundles in homes to bless mothers and newborns. In larger saining rituals, livestock would be driven between bonfires, usually lit with juniper, yew, and pine, and people would jump through or over them. Animals would be sained with medicinal herbs to heal them from illness. Folk would sometimes carry home embers from these fires to light their hearth fires and bless their home. Saining was also done with blessed water. In the New Year's Hogmanay customs, this is still done today. We cannot equate Saining to a Smudging Ceremony, or energetic smoke bowl cleansing, as these practices aren't easily swapped one for the other and are mutually and culturally exclusive.

Ancient Egyptians made their specially blended kyphi incense for thousands of years, and it is still made and used today. This is a compound blend of ingredients ground and mixed together to form chunks. The combination of ingredients contains ingredients such as (but not limited to) cinnamon, lemongrass, cedar, juniper berries, sage, cardamom, gum mastic, myrrh, frankincense, among many others. The traditional base of kyphi is honey, fruit, and wine.

Eastern traditions in India and Asia have well documented incense uses deriving from local plants and many combinations of these for much the same purposes as seen worldwide. Of course, most of us know that the Bible and Torah are filled with accounts of medicinal herbs and resins and their importance in those cultures. Not the least of which is the very famous story of Jesus' birth, and the gifts of frankincense and myrrh. As we know, these resins are still burned today in the Catholic churches, and many of us are very familiar with the intoxicating aroma. Herbs are medicine, as all ancient cultures knew, and fortunately that knowledge has not been lost. We can all benefit from a return to some of this ancient knowledge.

In our modern times, humans have strayed far away from the natural gifts of our planet, that people just don't understand these things anymore, unfortunately. Many of us have noticed a bit of a shift in regards to people having a great interest, as well as a need, for natural foods and medicines, and spirituality. This also includes a back to nature approach for many and a yearning for that which has been lost by so many over the years of "progress." Science is coming to terms with what so many indigenous peoples, empaths and sensitives, witches, herbalists, and neo-pagans already understand about energy and how it works, in the study of quantum physics. We now have an understanding that everything is made of vibrating energy, surrounded by an electromagnetic field of energy (what is sometimes termed as "aura") and that energy cannot be destroyed. When an organic being dies, their energy does not die with them, it simply takes another form. One does not need to have but a basic understanding of this to know that energy fields can be affected by outside influences, whether "positive" or "negative." I put these words into quotations, because energy really isn't positive/negative, dark/light, bad/good, etc., it just is. Storms, air purifiers, and salt lamps, for example, emit negative ions, which are good for us. The basic difference is simply vibration. Low vibration energy is considered by some to be "bad," "heavy," or "dark," whereas high vibration energy can be considered by some to be "good," or "light." It always feels better to vibrate at a higher frequency of positivity and light, of course, rather than to dwell at the low end of the spectrum. It is good to remember, however, that we are having a human experience here and that we have a need to experience all the expressions of frequency that we are able. It is natural, normal, and human to do so, and if one is having a "low energy day," it is natural and should be acknowledged. Energy is cyclical.

I am an Animist, a Pagan, and a practicing witch on an early modern traditional path. I am also a Reiki Master Teacher. Animism in my own daily life, healing practice, and spiritual path gives me the understanding that everything I see and touch has an energy field, and some kind of consciousness. I talk to inanimate objects and plants all the time. Do they talk back? In an extremely subtle fashion and in their own way, yes they do. In my yard, as well as walks in the woods, I try to drop into sensation awareness of my own body, and then the area in which I walk. When I do this, I notice subtle energies around me. I can feel if I feel welcome there that day, or when the spirits of place are less than friendly, which has happened. I do most of the time try to speak softly and introduce myself, and ask the beings who dwell there that no harm come to me and to see me as a friend. I leave a bit of my herbs or flowers as an offering and pour some water from my bottle. When I can, I try to give these at the base of a large tree. Sometimes, there are what I call Guardian Trees, the really big old ones, and give these majestic spirits the offerings, touch them, and say hello. When I enter with respect, I intend for the land spirits, trees, animals, rocks, and plants to notice this and hopefully let me pass. Most times, I will always come home with a gift just for me from Nature, some of which weren't there on the path into the woods but are sitting there for me to notice on my way out. I always bring trash bags to pick up any litter I see and carry it out with me. Never leave anything but footprints in Nature, and don't tie things to trees that could kill a branch or choke an animal if left there. Please don't leave offerings that could make the land or an animal sick, like salt and food items other than raw fruits or vegetables, and never take anything from a place without asking first, preferably leaving an offering and a thank you! You do not have to consider yourself an Animist or a Pagan to have animistic and respectful daily practices. But, if you are on a walk to wildharvest plants, get permission from the plant, leave an offering of water or something else biodegradable, and only take part of the plant. Please see the Chapter 4 on Wildharvesting, and do no harm.

It must be stated that regardless of the methods of herbal cleansing that appeal to you and that you decide to adopt as practice, you must honor and understand the cultures, traditions, and peoples that came before you or have shared with you their knowledge. In other words, if you are a non-indigenous person burning white sage or palo santo, for example, please have respect and understanding of where in the world these plants come from, which cultures they are attributed to, and their properties. Never misappropriate indigenous cultures and adopt their sacred dress and ceremony. Respect for other peoples and their cultures is paramount. That being said, similar plants grow around the world, and even in ancient times, our ancestors traded with other cultures, and some traditions are a syncretization of some older traditions and blending of cultures, the origins of which have occasionally been lost to time. If there are incenses and herbs you are curious about, try them! If at any time you feel uncomfortable using certain ingredients or doing any kind of practice or ritual and it doesn't sit right somehow, then don't do them again, or maybe swap out one herb for another that may resonate with you a bit more. For example, if you feel uneasy using white sage, pick an herb with similar properties and use that instead. I know many people are trying to shed outdated ideas and world views and are trying to live their lives a bit more authentically to find their own sense of place and belonging. This can be hard for some of us who do not live anywhere near the places of the world where our ancestors hailed from, if we even know who they are. For these reasons, it seems we are lost at times with little connection to our ancestors' cultures leaving us with no knowledge of their history. It is perfectly alright to use readily available items in your own practices, to try and experiment in the privacy of your own home, but please make them your own, while having the utmost reverence and respect for those who came before you, as well as honor for the plants themselves.

Some people do not have much connection to their ancestry, or have a few cultures represented in their family, and we may simply identify as inhabitants of the country we were born in. This is prevalent in the USA, which is wonderfully known as a beautiful melting pot of races, cultures, and spiritual traditions from all over the world. We may want to use the herbs that are native to our continent, because this is where we call Home. But if the history of colonization that came with Europeans is problematic for you, as it is for many, consider this. See how you can connect with your Ancestors' heritage, read about these places, their cultures and history, and the plants and foods that grow there. Look up your ancestry with a DNA service, if you aren't sure. Understand that many plants grow in many countries around the world and it is ok to use them as your ancestors did, and that this may look quite similar to practices of people who live on the other side of the world. Sweetgrass is a good example, as it is not only sacred to indigenous Native Americans, but also to Scandinavians, and very easily grown in many places worldwide. Rosemary and lavender are such wonderful and beloved healer plants, also easily grown in many gardens throughout the world, that no one should have any qualms about using. If you live in an area you can grow the herbs you like and resonate with, use them, these are yours, you grew them with your own hands and lots of love, use them for whatever purpose you choose! Use your own discernment and be sure to eschew the use of any material that you do not feel comfortable using, as this could change the energy you are adding to your mix.

Courtney, a lovely friend of mine, has Slovenian ancestry. She told me her family's story about their own Yule ritual of house blessing, which included her grandmother creating pine bundles, lighting them, and dispersing the smoke around the home, to bless it and the inhabitants. This is a pre-Christian practice, which morphed over time to include filling a pan loaded with charcoal, evergreens and woods, and asperging with an evergreen twig dipped in holy water to ensure the next year is filled with prosperity. In this way, people bless their property, fields, and animals for abundance and good harvest in the year to come. Another friend of mine, Janara, moved to California to work as a ski instructor. I received an unexpected package from her one day, only to have found inside a bag full of fresh and beautiful evergreen leaves for my incense, full of spruce and cedar. This came from a pristine and clean source high in the Sierras, and I cherished it and was grateful for this beautiful mountain energy, and thought of her and the amazing place in which she lives when I burned it.

The Science of Smudging

All that man needs for health and healing has been provided by God in nature, the challenge of science is to find it.

~ Paracelsus

Fortunately, modern science is catching on to the fact that burnable herbs and resins have many healing and antimicrobial properties. Our ancestors already knew this, regardless of whether they knew what microbes actually were, or the causes of pain or disease. They did know that certain herbs when burned as incenses can keep sickness and disease at bay. As stated in the previous chapter, smoke was used in sick rooms, hospitals, at funerals and in embalming practices, etc. to purify the air, the ill, and the dead of contagions. Spiritual and energetic properties aside, this is one more amazing reason to utilize smoke cleansing, especially during and after illness. We smudge our home and ourselves when others have been over that have been ill with colds or flus, and if we ourselves are feeling like we may be coming down with something. We really do feel that this works for us. Please enjoy the herbs and resins chapters for more information on some of the recommended plants' healing properties.

Medical science's advancements into our modern age contain some of the most powerful medicines and procedures. Medications have been developed from the plant kingdom, some synthesized into powerful and life-saving remedies. Plants heal! In the world of incenses, some of the benefits attributed to certain herbs and resins, especially sage, frankincense, and myrrh, include antiseptic, antifungal and anti-inflammatory, antidepressant, antimicrobial and antiviral, astringent, expectorant, stimulant, carminative, stomachic, anti-catarrhal, anti-spasmodic, immune boosting, and can stimulate circulation. As we know, many microbes are airborne from sneezing and coughing, as well as transmitted from hands and stationary objects. Researchers at Cardiff University, Wales, UK, have found that frankincense is a powerful anti-inflammatory, especially with arthritis pain.[2] Many believe that the gifts of the Magi to the baby Jesus were practical in nature, as well as spiritual, in regard to the healing properties of these resins. There have been studies done in controlled settings with burnables where it was clearly seen that the smoke from these killed microbes in the air and in vitro.[3] If this interests you, please read the studies referenced in the endnotes.

As you can see, wisdom of the ancients is much more than "old wives' tales" or stories in history books. There is much more information out there in books and the internet to back up these scientific studies and the claims of those who have used these substances in healing. I encourage you to delve deeper if this information resonates with you and do your own homework. It really is quite fascinating how so many members of the plant kingdom work hand in hand with the animal kingdom for health and healing. There is no such thing as a weed, everything has a reason for being in the grand scheme of things. A weed is just a plant for whom a purpose has not yet been found!

Chapter 2

What Is Energetic Smudging?

Amber and myrrh, benzoin and musk condense
To transports of the spirit and the sense!
~ Charles Baudelaire translated by Allen Tate

As we know from the previous chapter, smudging is a system of energetic cleansing for your body, mind, spirit, and physical items. Everything has an energy field and a spirit, including beings in the plant kingdom. It is said that certain plants are helpers of the animal kingdom, and are here for the purpose of some form of healing. You may know that certain herbs and spices are not only used for seasoning your food, but were adopted for this purpose because of their healing properties. For example, the scientific analysis of the properties of spicy health powerhouses called "superfoods," such as cayenne, garlic, turmeric, black pepper, ginger, rosemary, cinnamon, cumin, etc. made us aware that these foods are healing for our bodies, as well as just simply delicious added to our foods. While many herbs for ingesting aren't suitable for burning, you get the idea that many of nature's gifts have healing purposes whether ingested in the form of food or drink, turned into essential oils, or burning as incenses.

What energetic clearing does is clean your energy field, like soap cleans your body. Think of it as an etheric practice akin to your daily bath...a smoke bath. Just as you wash your physical body and hands every day, you will be bathing your energetic body with herbal smoke. If you think of all the goo, grime, dust, and dirt that sticks to you by the end of the day, you will understand that the same thing goes for your energy field. Imprints of energy can be somewhat insidious, in that, you pick up "goo" if you will, from every person and every "thing" you have come in contact with that day. You can pick up all kinds of vibrations and energy, sometimes "positive" and affirming, but many more that are low vibration or "negative". My (and many others) belief is that these can stick to you like mud, and may affect your energy and moods. People who were in your home and touched your things also will leave an "imprint" behind. This can be ameliorated by a simple daily, weekly, or monthly practice of cleansing with incense, not only your body, but also your home. I generally try to smudge my body weekly, or before a ritual, the entirety of my home monthly, and definitely after returning home from being away, such as vacation.

If people have been in your home, it is a good idea to clear as well as clean after they leave. Smudge things you buy, doors and windowsills, most definitely your bed, pillows, computer, phone, etc. as often as possible. Consider it good hygiene for your energy field. You will most definitely notice a big difference in your vibration if you make this a practice on a regular basis, as this not only cleans you of heavy, stagnant energy, but attracts light and joyful energy. Remember that cleansing is a continuous process, just like you would clean your home weekly, and energetic hygiene should be a regular practice in your life. This also extends to keeping your home cleaned and decluttered. The first practice you should do even before energetically cleansing your home is to physically clean it, especially when you are feeling low energy, "stuck," or stagnant. Get that energy moving again! No amount of incense replaces some semblance of cleanliness and order. Living in chaos, filth, disarray, and too much "stuff" everywhere creates disorder in your life as well as your thoughts. This doesn't mean that you should stress over constant "protection" or things being constantly attached to you. This is everyone's daily situation. It is only a problem when disorder permeates you or your space and you do not take steps to address it.

On a personal note, a home in which I used to live was placed upon the land by me, so was brand new at the time I moved in a number of years ago. However, since the very beginning of my residence there, it had been plagued by very low and dark energy, spirit activity, and general strangenesses. Without getting into too much detail, suffice it to say, my son and I were even creeped out about going outside into the backyard at night. Once I started a regular smudging practice as well as my Reiki healing practices, the dark and malevolent-feeling energies dissipated over time and left the premises. I also cleansed the perimeter of the property outside, and used charged crystals in the home's corners to anchor some protection and light energy. Regardless of what went on upon this land over time (there is also either an earth ley line that cuts through the house or a liminal space/portal in this spot), I kept the weirdness at bay by using multiple tools at my disposal, including Himalayan salt lamps.

All spiritual paths are compatible with the addition of an herbal incense smoke bowl. Many people already incorporate the burning of special or sacred herbs upon their altar or sacred space during rituals. As the wheel of the year turns and many of us observe spiritual holidays, celebrations, and historical observances such as Beltaine, Samhain, or Yule, these occasions are perfect for doing an energetic cleansing of yourself, loved ones, and your home. You can use this practice to clear chaotic energy from your home, after rearranging and changing decor to fit the seasons and special occasions, and is most welcome after doing a house cleaning. Cleanse your space with fragrant, herbal smoke after doing the hard work, to "lay the dust" and neutralize chaotic energies, and invoke blessings, beneficial spirits, and high vibrations into your home.

Many of our favorite Spirit Allies and deities in the vast pantheon of gods and goddesses have plants and herbs of which they are fond, and many of us use some of these, although not all are suitable for burning, in our special observances, or keep them on our altars. Consider using an herb or resin incense that is special to them and can help you connect to their energy, and create a pathway to communication with them. Days of the week, Moon phases, and celestial happenings as well may influence what you decide to place on an altar, or burn in a censer. On an ancestor and family altar, for example, I keep rosemary (for remembrance), as well as a dish filled with my own special blend of sage, lavender, cedar, juniper, sweetgrass, and yerba santa to burn as an offering to my family. Sacred smoke is more than just clearing, many see smoke as a messenger to the divine upon which prayers, petitions, and blessings can be carried. Be sure to pay attention to the path smudge smoke creates, it's swirls and eddies around objects, and how it behaves during smudging a home. Interesting smoke patterns and quantity of smoke can be indicators of the presence of an entity or simply a deep need for a clearing of someone or something's energy field.

Since this is a book on herbal cleansing, I won't go into much detail about other methods of energetic cleansing and raising vibrations, of which there are many. Clearing and protection can also be done with crystals, Himalayan salt lamps, uplifting music, singing/chanting, drumming, and bell ringing (See Chapter 8). Try a combination of all of these things, the atmosphere in your home will benefit, I guarantee!

How to Smudge

Energetic smoke cleansing can be as simple or as complicated and ritualistic as you decide to make it. There are basics to the process, however, no hard and fast rules. You may hear from others that you are doing something the wrong way, or they may try to have you do things their way or in their tradition. Honor their input, but make up your own mind, as this is your path. If you are smudging another person, you may wish to ask them if they have a method they prefer, so as to make them more comfortable. If you belong to a specific heritage, religion or spiritual path, ethnic group, or have relatives from certain areas of the world with specific smoke cleansing rituals, this possibly may be the way you will choose to do things. For another, this may be completely different. Only you can choose the types of herbs and plant material you wish to use, and the ways in which you use them. It's always fun to experiment to see which ones you connect with, and please feel free to add your own styles and twists to the process. This process should be taken seriously and with the highest intentions, however, not to the point that you don't feel you can place your own personal stamp of expression on it. Simple and direct is the best, until you can memorize the steps easily without looking at complicated notes while doing so.

Many indigenous people's traditions require one to start the smoke bath at the feet and work your way upward. Other traditions require the smoke bath to start at the chest and upward, then down toward the feet. If you are familiar with the chakra energy points of the body, you may want to smudge each of these specifically. Chakra points are vortexes of energy that spin, and are located in relation to, and communicate with, the biological systems of your body, including the endocrine and nervous systems. Sometimes these chakras (and resulting glands or organs) can be out of balance. A regular smudging practice can help balance these. Those that are aware of chakras know about the seven chakras: Root, Sacral, Solar Plexus, Heart, Throat, Forehead, Crown, but may not recognize that the body has many more chakra points. There are energy points in the palms of the hands, as well as the soles of the feet, so be sure to smudge these as well. These points are especially important, as the feet touch the earth, and the hands touch everything, including objects throughout your day, your family members, pets, and food. Be sure your hands are clean with the smoke, just as you do when washing in soap and water. In my personal practice when I am able to do a thorough cleansing of my body, I start first with my hands and "wash" them in the smoke. I then run my arms through the smoke. I pick up the censer (I use either an abalone shell, a soapstone bowl, or a beautiful clay copalera that was a very special gift from a friend), then waft the smoke with a feather toward my heart, up to my throat, face, over my head, down the left side of my body to my feet, smudge the soles of my feet, continue up the right side of my body, then run the smoke up behind and up my body from the back. Doing the feet and back can be a bit hard, so be careful. If someone else is present, have them smudge you, then return the favor.

Simply fan the smoke over you, your object, or the room you are in with the feather or a feather fan to cleanse. It is also just fine to just use your hand if no feather is available, or walk around with the smoking herbs and waft them into rooms, etc. When you are finished, if at all possible, open a few windows to give the smoke and energy an outlet and bring in some fresh air. Direct smoke with your hands, or the preferred method, a feather* or feather fan. It is also fun to use feathers that you may find in your yard or on a walk in the woods. I consider these gifts from the Bird People, and collect many of them. Remember that some feathers are illegal in certain countries to own. Commercially available feathers are usually always from domestic fowl such as turkeys, chickens, peacocks, etc.

To smudge a home, it is best to leave windows closed during the cleansing process. The reason for this is to concentrate the smoke in each room for a few minutes for maximum effectiveness. When finished, open or at least crack the windows to give the smoke and energy an outlet. Where to start in the home may depend upon a certain tradition, however, once again, feel free to experiment to see what your preferences are. Many people start in the East of the house, and walk through the home clockwise, ending up back at the same spot. Some start at the front door and end up back at this point. I have also heard of people that start in the kitchen because it is the "heart of the house." Once again, use your own intuition! Walk into each room wafting smoke as you go, say a personal blessing if needed. When in each room, pay particular attention to the corners and closets, as stagnant energy can accumulate there. Waft smoke around the windows and doors. Say a thank you to the smoke in the room and continue to the next. Be sure to cleanse all of the doors and windows in the home. Pay particular attention to your bedroom. We are vulnerable in this room, especially during our sleep time, and need to keep this room high vibration. Cleanse your bed, pillows, bedding, under your bed if able, as well as your closet, as this can sometimes become stagnant when kept closed. Cleanse desks, computers, and electronic equipment especially. Have fun with it, no matter what, and do not take yourself too seriously. See the *Powerful Prayers and Rewarding Rituals* chapter for more details and ritual ideas.

I once had someone try to tell me to never smudge in the bathrooms because it would dishonor the spirits because what is done in the bathrooms is not "clean." I wholeheartedly disagree with this statement! There are many ways one can annoy a spirit, but burning incense in the bathroom is not one of them. The Spirits know we are weirdos in human skin suits and have special biological needs that they do not have. In my opinion, the bathroom is one place that definitely needs it because when one is in this room we are at our most vulnerable. Whether answering nature's call or bathing, there is no other time, except while sleeping, that we are more exposed. This room can have some low vibrations in it, and benefits from occasional smoke bath. Cleanse your sinks, toilets, bathtubs, and inside the shower stall. If you don't have a window to open in your bathroom and have a fan, use it to clear the smoke a few minutes after you are finished. However, try to avoid using herbs as just an air freshener, and if you feel you need one, maybe just use an incense stick. As a side note, many people are aware that bath time seems to be a time when the veil thins a bit and one can get divine insights and inspirations. Creativity and sudden ideas or inspirations have happened to us as well at this time. There are a few theories in regard to this, however, keep the bath area high vibe, and you never know what great inspirations may pop into your head when you least expect it, this has most definitely happened to me! As always, scrub your bathroom. Want a high vibe home? Honor it by keeping it clean and germ-free.

Objects in your home that are new to you should always need to be cleansed. Remember that energy has "substance" like dirt and germs do, regardless of if it can be seen with the naked eye or not. Everyone that has come in contact with that item has left an imprint behind, like an energetic fingerprint. This includes the people that made the materials that are included in your object, the factory workers, the packers and shippers, the employees at the store in which it was purchased, as well as customers that have touched it in the store. If anyone was under the weather, angry, or depressed, they can leave these imprints on your item. The more sensitive you are to energy fields, the more you can sense this. It doesn't matter at all if you cannot sense this energy, just know and trust that it is there. If your mood suddenly changes for what seems to be little reason after holding or touching something, or being near to someone with very high or very low energy, you know this can be a direct result of their energy. Your goal is to neutralize things you bring into your home, which is your very own sacred space. To cleanse objects, especially new items you have purchased or had given to you as gifts, waft smoke over the object or, if it is small, pass it through the smoke.

Smudging Specifics

There are many different types of herbs, woods, and tree resins used in smudging practices, and different ways to burn them.

Bundled herbs in wand or stick form, as well as sticks of wood, are easy and ones which you may be familiar already, such as the white sage smudge stick or palo santo wood. To burn these, simply hold the stem end of the bundle and light the end with a lighter or flame. Let the bundle flame for a few seconds then blow out the flame if it has not gone out on its own, which it frequently will. The tip of the bundle will be glowing and emitting fragrant smoke now, and this is what you will use to smudge. A good way to use this method is to lay the stick in a vessel that you can carry in one hand, such as an abalone shell. You can hold both of these in one hand and a feather* in another (if using) to disperse the smoke. Be very, very careful when using this method, as embers will fall from the end of the bundle, which is why some use the shell/bundle method to catch any burnt bits and embers which may fall. If doing a longer session, you may re-light the bundle to continue. Sage bundles and palo santo wood can be re-lit many times, and are long-lasting. Bundles can be laid down in a heat-proof vessel, dish, censer, or shell when finished, and should go out on their own if somewhat fresh. Vessels for burning incense are sometimes called braziers or censers, regardless of the material they are made of (I consider braziers to be the very large bowls

* A word about feathers: If using bird feathers, please be aware that ownership of certain feathers is illegal in the U.S. These include, but are not limited to protected species such as eagles, hawks, owls and other raptors. The only persons that are allowed to have feathers such as these are indigenous Native Americans who have the proper documentation on where they have purchased them. Even finding a protected dead bird on the side of the road and harvesting its feathers is against the law. The only feathers able to be legally used are domestic fowl and meat birds such as turkeys, roosters, pheasants, partridge, etc. There are many beautiful feather fans that I, as well as others make to sell. Please be sure that the person you buy one from knows their feathers. You do not need to be fined or jailed because of someone else's ignorance. See the Migratory Bird Treaty of 1918. MBTA prohibits the taking (including killing, capturing, selling, trading, and transport) of protected migratory bird species without prior authorization by the Department of Interior U.S. Fish and Wildlife Service.[4]

with legs usually placed outside). Older bundles can be very dry, and may not go out on their own, so keep an eye on these. Watch them carefully after laying them down, and never leave a burning charcoal or sage bundle unattended! We were vending at a festival and lit a sage bundle to purify our booth. We laid the bundle down thinking it was out and a few minutes later, it came back to life, flames and all! I learned from this mistake, and it will never be repeated.

Loose herbs and tree resins will be burned on a charcoal tablet. These tablets can be found in metaphysical shops, tobacco shops, religious supply houses, and of course, the internet, and are usually sold as hookah charcoals. Charcoal comes in various sizes, you can experiment with these and you will find you may need different sizes in your home for quick smudges, and larger ones for house blessings. I recommend using small tongs to hold the tablet while you run the flame from a lighter or candle around the edges of it. These should start to sparkle and glow a bit when they are properly lit, then lay the tablet in the vessel to continue to light. Light the charcoal disk, and when it ashes over to gray, much like charcoal does on a grill, place herbs or resins directly on the charcoal. You can use a standard sized hookah charcoal for 15 minutes or so. If you need to "reload" it with fresh incense, you can scrape away the burnt bits to the side, as these may start to give a very burnt smell depending upon the plant used. Be sure to place sand or small gravel at the bottom of the shell or vessel to protect it and keep the bottom from getting too hot. This will protect your furniture and possibly your hands, as well. Some folks (myself included) use a wooden tripod stand to place the shell on to keep it off of the furniture.

Safety First!

Please be sure to use caution while burning herbs in any fashion. Much like you would take care when lighting candles and open flames, take these precautions with lit smudging herbs, as well.

Be sure to place sand or small gravel in the bottom of your smudging bowl to protect your hands and your furniture, or leave a bed of ash for your coal to rest on. Long hair should be tied up if possible. Be extra careful with flowing clothing and accessories, billowy sleeves and outfits pose an extra hazard when working with burning bowls and flames. It is preferable to not wear these clothes if there is some concern. As with candle flames, do not place burning smudge vessels near curtains or anything that can catch fire. Always keep an eye out for your pets, especially cats, that can brush tails and whiskers into embers or knock your vessel over. Be sure that your coals are completely out and cold before you dispose of them, just as you would with barbecue grill embers or fireplace ashes. Never walk away from a burning incense bowl!

It is not recommended to smudge if you are pregnant or smudge a pregnant person. Many herbs and plants, like mugwort, can be dangerous and cause bleeding or miscarriage. Very young children and babies also should not be exposed to herbal smoke. Some traditions also exclude from these practices women who are in the time of their moon for other reasons we won't delve into here. Be careful of smoke cleansing around people with severe allergies or respiratory issues, or do this outside.

It must be stated to enter into this practice with a clear, sound mind, and solid intentions. It is not a good idea to smudge, or do any ritual or spiritual work while under the influence of drugs or alcohol. Having clouded judgment can cause accidents, cloud the intentions of the work, lower your vibration, and if you are working with Spirit Allies, can be a sign of disrespect.

Smudging the Garden and Property

As I stated previously, I smudge the property upon which I live occasionally, as well as my garden areas. Walking the perimeter of your land with smoke or with just dried herbs, creates a sacred space, clears, raises the vibration, offers protection to your family, and can be an offering to the land spirits and elementals that live there. This should be done periodically, but is not necessary on a frequent basis unless you have some major clearing work to do there. A great time to do this is during a New Moon phase, as a New Moon denote cleansing, rebirth, and renewal. Other auspicious times (if you resonate with such) can be our quarterly Equinoxes and Solstices, Full Moon times to anchor positivity and power, or if banishing low energy, the waning and Dark Moon period is also suggested. Regardless, there is no right or wrong way, especially if you are feeling the need to smudge your area. Just do it! Be very careful, of course, of burning embers setting leaves and garden debris afire.

Many people also smudge their garden areas, the plants love it! Older plantings can benefit from some renewed energy and everything seems to grow a bit happier. I can also recommend placing one sage leaf or a chunk of your favorite resin in the planting hole with a new plant. If you have loose herbs, feel free to bless them and strew them about the garden to return to the earth with good intentions.

Strewing Herbs

It has been a practice in older times to strew herbs upon the floor of a home, and some folks do this today. The reasons for this are many-fold: to repel insects, vermin, and illness, keep odors at bay (especially in the days when people didn't bathe or clean regularly), insulation and cushioning before the days of carpets, as well as for simple fragrance and uplifting moods. In these days and times, cleanliness is an obsession. The overuse of chemical cleaning agents and synthetic air fresheners is appalling and very unhealthy. There is also evidence to suggest that some of these chemicals can be cancer-causing agents. Try some natural alternatives for a healthier home.

If you are plagued with insects such as spiders, fleas, moths, or ants, try anything in the mint family, thyme, lavender, as well as cedar shavings, which smell amazing and insects flee from these herbs. Rosemary, bay leaves, and cooking sage kill insects. Make sachets of your smudging herbs to freshen closets, drawers, pillows, mattresses, etc. Why not use nature's potpourri not just in dishes, but give the floors a thorough strewing with herbs and flowers. Do not use fresh herbs. Be sure these are well dried, natural and not enhanced with any extra fragrances, and not artificially colored, so as to not stain floors and carpets, or create a mold problem as fresh herbs decay. Walk on them then vacuum or sweep them up on your cleaning day, then place outside for the earth or garden to compost. Instead of purchasing artificially-scented rug freshening powders, make your own with finely ground herbs mixed with corn meal. Sprinkle on carpets, wait awhile, then vacuum normally. Some folks recommend using baking soda, however, this is very fine powder and some vacuum cleaners with HEPA filters can become clogged with the dust. Coarser corn meal is a better choice if you go the carpet powder route, otherwise, use the herbs by themselves.

Simmering Herbs

Most safe dried herbs can be used as potpourri or in simmer pots. Simmering herbs on the stove on the warm setting can infuse a home with beautiful and natural scents, unlike air fresheners and sprays, which are generally regarded as being potentially allergenic or harmful over periods of time, especially for pets. Many people use cinnamon sticks, oranges, lemons, cloves, etc. simmered in water, especially around the holidays or when selling a home. You can do this same practice with your smudging herbs! Feel free to add in citrus and other spices like cinnamon and cloves. I do this often, and you can usually get a few simmers out of a pot of herbs and fruit before it gets a bit spent. Be sure to use a dedicated and small basic cooking pot for this and keep other ones just for your food, I have a very old one I no longer cook in for this purpose. Be sure there is enough water in the pot and set it to low or warm setting. Keep an eye on the water level so it does not boil away and burn. Never leave the house with your stove warming a simmer pot, just as you would not walk away from your burning incense.

Chapter 3

Powerful Prayers and Rewarding Rituals

Oh Great Spirit who made all races, look kindly upon the whole human family and take away the arrogance and hatred that separates us from our brothers.

~ Cherokee Prayer

Prayers or mantras are always encouraged, as words have great power. The sky is the limit when it comes to uplifting and encouraging statements you can include in your practices, but have fun with writing your own. When you write your own, it can be a simple on-the-spot and spontaneous thing, or you can write and memorize a longer, more elaborate mantra. I frequently make up little rhymes while I am doing energetic work, as well as blessing items and doing other things, while I am in the moment and don't write them down. What comes to you sometimes is all you need for that particular time. The more "you" that is included, the more meaningful and powerful this practice will become. You can start out by reciting a prayer you may have found in a book or online, or even recited to you by an elder or friend, then re-word it and make it uniquely your own. Affirmations and prayers that rhyme feel great and flow smoothly from the tongue, and also are able to be sung (I am a vocalist and love to use a sing-song voice when I recite mantras and blessings, it makes it fun and easy to remember, but can be powerful).

Here are a few basic sweet ones that I wrote, feel free to use them, but even better add your own words specific to your situation and/or choice of deity. Very personal ones with my specific Spirit Allies I keep to myself.

Blessed plants do your work; Your healing duties do not shirk; Vibrations high, energy clean; Banish negativity, So Mote It Be

During illness I use Frankincense and came up with this variation:

Frankincense, Frankincense do your work; your healing powers do not shirk; Keep me healthy, keep me clean; I Am well and whole, Blessed Be

One for everyday smudging:

I banish all negativity; Happy vibes surrounding me; Carry smoke upon the winds; to the skies on wispy wings

An ancient Greek phrase from the Eleusinian Mysteries is one I use quite frequently to cleanse and clear, including at my altar and before my own rituals:

Hekas hekas este bebeloi" means "Far, far from this place be the profane!" It is pronounced "eh-kaas eh-kaas es-tay beh beh loy

The beautiful smudging prayer below has been floating around awhile, and I am not sure of the origins. I received it from the Chopra Center:[5]

May your hands be cleansed, that they create beautiful things.
May your feet be cleansed, that they might take you where you most need to be.
May your heart be cleansed, that you might hear its messages clearly.
May your throat be cleansed, that you might speak rightly when words are needed.

May your eyes be cleansed, that you might see the signs and wonders of the world.
May this person and space be washed clean by the smoke of these fragrant plants."
And may that same smoke carry our prayers, spiraling, to the heavens.

The Tibetan Buddhist mantra *Om Mani Padme Hum* or the Green Tara mantra *Om Tare Tuttare Ture Soha* while doing this work invokes compassion, blessings, and peace. These calm, soothe, and comfort me. I have a special mantra I keep to myself, the words nonsensical (or are they?), however, it is powerfully calming to me. Feel free to create your own special prayers and mantras. It matters not that they have meaning to anyone else but you.

I have a special interest in Heathenism and Norse Paganism, and as I stated previously, I am an Animist, so I really love this special invocation the band Heilung[6] recites together onstage prior to their opening performance, as it creates awareness of our connection to All:

Remember, that we all are brothers
All people, beasts, trees and stone and wind
We all descend from the one great being
That was always there
Before people lived and named it
Before the first seed sprouted

Here is another beautiful one I found online from Hidden Hearth Witch:[7]

Hail to the Gods, hail to the Goddesses, hail to the Mighty, hail to the Wise.

Hail to the Earth, hail to the Sky, hail to the Sea with its ebb and flow.
Hail to the Sun, hail to the Moon, hail to the Stars that light up the Night.
Hail to our Ancestors, hail to our kin, hail to our friends, hail to our foes.
May the Gods bless us, may the Goddesses guide us, may the Spirits protect us.
May our deeds be honorable, may our words be true, may our hearts be brave.
So Be It.

Many of us will call upon a deity or deities, familiars, angels, guardians, our higher self, the ancestors, or a combination of these to appeal to during prayer, ask for their blessings and protection. If you feel a particular affinity for a specific spirit helper, by all means include them in your prayers and mantras. Change it up from time to time, and call upon others as the need develops. Some have multiple deities with which they work, and ask for help from different ones depending upon the work they are doing. This includes dear departed loved ones, as well.

It is perfectly okay to not include any prayers, mantras, or affirmations in your work. There are those that do not follow any spiritual path at all, but still understand the benefits of energy work and utilize these practices. Anyone can feel the difference in their energy field and how they are feeling after a nice bath with the smoke from a healing herb. After all, there really is science behind how this all works, as well as a magical feel at times.

Ritual

Creating ritual can be a fun and very rewarding part of your smoke cleansing practices. Personalizing these, adding a bit of flair and flourish, speaking words or mantras as you go, can elevate them to another level energetically. Sprinkle your smoke with a bit of magical flavor and add an air of otherworldliness, to keep you interested and engaged as you direct the smoke around you or into your space. You do not have to be a magical practitioner of any kind, an energy healer, or be a member of any religion or spiritual path in order to make this extra special for you. Energy currents swirl around us all day, every day. If you recognize this, know that you are a part of it all, a denizen of Earth, and a contributing member of the world of living things, which means you are attached to it all, this is your birthright! As we stand in our own power, we make it known and reclaim our power as functioning members of this immense web of life. We are set firmly in the middle of everything, on equal footing with all living things, neither above, below, inferior, or superior to anyone.

Energetically aware people, whether witches, Reiki practitioners/ healers and therapists, or animistic pagans, have methods for connecting to these energetic currents, drawing them in and utilizing them for their own purposes. While doing this, we are also adding our own signature to the delicious soup that is the field of energy in which we live and creating ripples just by existing. If you are reading this book, that means that you are also an energetically aware person ready to enlarge your understanding of the weird world around you. Atheists and agnostics can also have this understanding, and may choose to approach it from a scientific standpoint, knowing that many plants are medicine and that energy fields are very, very real! Smudging works for anyone and everyone, regardless of belief systems. Whether you change, clear, charge, or move energy, know that what you are doing is working on some level, even if you cannot see or feel it.

There may be some people who are concerned because they have trouble visualizing, or have some neurodivergence which may prevent them from focusing or sitting still for long, and are now sure how to approach any energy related practices. Some folks may not have the ability to concentrate deeply on ritual or do much meditation or mindfulness exercises. This does not matter to any kind of energy work, including smudging. If this includes you or someone you know, just know that this will work for you, and create the outcome that you desire. Herbs and plants do not depend upon you being able to visualize their energy or even what they look like in their natural growing life. They will do their work regardless of us and our opinions of it all! On a personal note, I have a close friend who is also a Reiki Master Teacher. He is aphantasic, which means that he does not have an inner dialogue or a way to visualize in his mind's eye any symbols or concepts relating to creating "mind pictures." He is not able to follow along with a guided meditation with visualizations, see shapes or images when called upon to do so, or see the Reiki symbols in his mind at all. He just simply knows that what he does will work. He can draw them with his hands and that is good enough for him, and he has the ability to transfer attunements to students, as well as practice healing on others, and it works perfectly wonderfully!

Grounding, Centering and Shielding:

Many of you reading this may already know about grounding and centering, and may do this on a regular basis. Many of you may be new to all of this, or possibly have heard of grounding, but are not sure exactly what it entails, or why one would need to do this. I will talk briefly about a couple different ways to ground and center, and very highly recommend that everyone does this daily, if not at least very regularly. This exercise should always be done before a smoke cleansing, or ritual of any kind, in my opinion.

Have you ever had a day that just seems a bit off for you, or nothing seems to be going the way you intend? Maybe things keep breaking, you are bumping into things, stubbing your toes, or bumbling around feeling like not much is being accomplished today? Maybe others are speaking to you, but you can't concentrate, or their energy is rubbing you the wrong way? Are you tired, stressed, feeling "airy fairy?" We all need a good grounding every now and again! Let's go over some basic grounding exercises now.

A great grounding and centering exercise many people know and use daily involves rooting to the earth. An ideal situation would involve you touching grass or dirt with your bare feet to really feel the connection, however, you can visualize yourself grounding and touching the earth, even if you are in a high-rise building in the middle of a city. You don't have to be in a forest or rural place to ground and center. Any time during any day you can do this basic visualization and it absolutely helps return you to the present moment fully in your body. Busy and stressful day at work? Go to an office or even a bathroom, touch a houseplant if you feel guided to, and ground. On your lunch break? Touch the grass outside your building, or find a little park if there is one, connect with some nature if at all possible. Kick off your shoes if you can, but this is not always possible. Remember, anyone can do this work, regardless of where you are, your visualization prowess, or lack thereof!

Stand (or sit, if standing is not an option) with your back straight, but relaxed. Both feet firmly on the ground, do not lock knees and keep your joints loose. Be comfortable, or you will concentrate on your discomfort more than the exercise. See cords coming from the bottoms of your feet and the base of your spine, feel these if you can, what does this look and feel like for you? Send these cords into the ground, even if it is many stories below your feet. Visualize them running deep, deep, deep into the heart of the Earth, through the topsoil, bedrock, Earth's crust, and on and on into the molten core at its center. Hear in your mind if possible, what it may sound like having these bust through solid rock (I "hear" them cracking and crunching as they go). I like to envision my cords as being blood red, my lifeblood, connecting to the lifeblood of Earth Mother, and snaking into a double helix on each cord. This is what is always has "looked" like for me, so this is what I use, but feel free to use whatever imagery works best for you. I then envision the core turning into a violet purple heart and see Her light coming back up through the cords, into my body, and into my own core. Sometimes when I have done this, I send a white cord from the top of my head into the sun or even the heart of the galaxy, and connect it with my heart and Earth's heart, if I really need an extra boost of strong healing energy. I intend for Earth to nourish me and ask her to ground and center me with her own Earth energies. Take as much or as little time you need to with this, when finished, thank Earth for her gift to you. You will feel better!

Another method involves using a tree to help you ground and center, because of their deep roots in the dark earth and the tops high up in the air and sunlight. They are tall and strong, heavy and solid, and very present in our reality. Trees can connect the underworld to the upper world, and are ideal for this practice. Some people believe trees are sentient and have individual personalities, so be sure to ask it if it's alright to share energy with it. Some are very used to humans and our energy and structures and may be more friendly, some don't have much connection with our human world at all, if you find them in an old forest or wilderness. You can stand and touch trees, or sit with your back against them (be sure there are no ant hills) and ground to your heart's content. I have the most beautiful old oaks around my house, they are all around 130 years old. One oak in particular is so big, I can stand on its thick roots, sometimes I actually do hug it and place my forehead upon it. I consider this tree to be my good friend, and ask it to anchor good vibrations in my home and property. I also leave my offerings after rituals at a crook in its roots and thank it for taking them to where they need to go. If you do this, please be sure these can't hurt wildlife or make anyone sick from eating perishable food, and never put salt on the earth. You can rub your hands together to start an energy flow (you don't have to be an energy healer to do this), place your hands on the bark, and you may be able to feel the tree's energies. You can do the same visualization as above, or simply stand there and ask the tree to take "bad" or low energy, sickness, sadness, or any miasmas or stress away from you, ground it to Earth and transmute it, and center you with "good" energy.

Just touching trees for a few minutes even without any visualization at all, can be very healing and grounding. Our business is called Tree Of Life, and I have a tree tattoo growing up the side of one of my legs. It makes me think of the World Tree, or Yggdrasil, the Tree Of Life in Norse mythology, as this is an interest and field of study of mine. As an energy-raising exercise, "see" its roots that you are also connected to in the heart of the earth, in the Underworld. Raise energy from the Lower World darkness and the deep wells at its base into your core, the Middle World; then up above you, snaking along your cords into the Upper World, and back down again into your center. With any method of grounding, you may have fun seeing and speaking to all the denizens of the Otherworlds as you are running up and down through the layers of reality. In other words, wave to the stone and crystal people on your way down, splash with the denizens of the waters in the underground streams, say hello to the earthworms and moles, flap your wings with the butterflies and birds as your energy ascends up to the skies!

No mention of grounding and centering, as well as any energy clearing, can be complete without mentioning shielding. Add an additional boost and layer of protection to yourself, your space, your home by sending up a shield when you are finished grounding and centering. Virtual shields are more than virtual, they really do work! The easiest way to do this is a quick technique I use and teach in my Reiki classes. "See" a white ball of light above your head, the exact placement of which is at the end of your fingertips if you put your hands together above your head. This can be called multiple things, some people call it your Soul Star chakra, or Wiracocha, but whatever you call it, it matters not. Poke this ball of energy with your fingertips, turn your palms outward and draw the white light down with your arms and underneath your feet, like you are pulling out a giant sheet from it to engulf you in a ball. This is your shield, if you can, see it and feel it in your mind's eye and body. You can visualize covering it with a mirror or chrome (helpful for sketchy or dangerous situations and people, or if you genuinely feel attacked), cover yourself with a "shield wall" like a Viking, you can fill it with the rainbow colors of your chakra system in layers, glittery healing sparkles, or fill it with a color that pleases you for any reason, or just shimmery white. When you are used to doing this, there may be a time when you can simply stand and concentrate for a minute to be present, then literally just say "Ground, Center, Shield!" If you wish, you can also have a statement such as "Protect me in my shield, allow only love to enter, for my greatest good" or anything to this effect to double down on your intentions. In an instant you are connected and shielded, that's all you have to do. This works well for me when I am not in my home, or if there is a lot of activity around me and I don't have time to spend visualizing anything more in depth. However, I do enjoy the extra time to really connect when I have a few extra minutes. There is much written about this, so we will not delve too deeply into it here, but know there are many, many methods of visualization about grounding, centering, and shielding practices, find the ones that make the most sense to you. Don't stress too much about shielding and protection constantly, especially if you do this on a regular basis. If you have good energetic hygiene and do regular work around it, you are pretty safe generally speaking. Most of the entities you need to protect yourself from are probably human, unfortunately.

More quick and fun methods to ground or uplift your energy are to touch houseplants, pets or other animals (animals are great because they are always grounded, and can share this with you); place some fresh herbs or flowers in your hands or even some grass; Hold rocks or crystals in your hands, these are obviously very connected to the deep earth; wash your hands in clear, cool water while visualizing any bad energy washing off and going down the drain (if you are feeling anxiety, cold water is fantastic for this, be sure to splash some on your face and neck if possible); shower cleansing by using the same method, but from your head to your toes, washing off old, stagnant energy away and visualizing yourself sparkling (I visualize the water changing into streams of healing golden white sparkles); have an aromatherapy session with natural herbs or genuine essential oils. Synthetic fragrances are not recommended for this simply because they are not for the most part made from natural materials, or they are so far removed from their original nature as to not have this connection in them, and can quite possibly be toxic.

I do not want to digress to much from the topics at hand, but I would like to take a moment to address intention. Whether you are doing tasks related to the mundane or magical, everything begins with intent. You may have heard or read that everything you do is "all about intention," which, of course, is very important, otherwise, how will you know the purpose of what you are about to do? However, in the energetic world, it takes more than just "good thoughts and positive intentions" to get work done. This is an extremely important first step, but you will need to do actual work to reach your goals. In other words, just lighting a candle or a sage bundle for a minute or two, and saying a few phrases when your mind is on other things, like getting to work or preparing dinner, isn't even remotely the same as focused intent and a clear purpose with an end result to concentrate on. In Reiki, we are taught to be unattached and let the energy do its work when we are connected to it and "in the flow," but otherwise when doing other work, including mundane tasks, it is good to have a real focus to your work. Another example may be when spiritual and religious people talk about the power of prayer, which when done with concentrated intention is very real and powerful, and may bring about the results they are looking for, especially when done repeatedly. In the occult world, this also applies, especially when doing workings on a regular basis for a specific goal. Just lighting some incense and wandering around for five minutes while thinking about other things, especially when stressed or tired, is not quite the same. In my opinion, taking the time, and possibly planning ahead for the right time of day to do a house blessing, for example, may be worth the extra effort. I learned at one time about a technique written by William S. Burroughs called Do Easy,[8] which I employ on a regular basis. There is also a fun video about it on the internet if you wish to look it up. It is a simple reminder to me to be present and mindful, so as to make your work flow, lessen mistakes, and eliminate accidents and it really works well for me. If I am lighting coals or candles, cutting vegetables for dinner, or walking down my stairs, if I remind myself of the simple phrase "Do Easy," my brain knows what to do. I am immediately brought back to focusing on the task at hand, which I believe can help keep me from cutting myself or tripping. Once DE is employed, or you're grounded and centered and in a good headspace, then you can get on with things! Just another little tidbit to share with you that helps me quite a bit.

House Blessing Ritual

Begin with a goal in mind. You may want to ask yourself some questions before you begin. Why are you cleansing your home? Does it need a blessing? Does your home need to have some extra sweet and fresh energy infused into it? Does your home need to have stagnant, chaotic energy eliminated from it? Are you needing more love, more luck, more or less of something? Are you having a party or observing a special holiday, birthday, a sabbat, or esbat? Some people love to do house blessing at the beginning of a new month, or on New Moons or Full Moons. Some may do a full ritual house cleansing and blessing quarterly, or at the New Year. You may want to consider the Moon phase you are in, as well as working with planetary hours. A Waxing Moon can be great for bringing something in, increasing, growing, things you want, energy you need, etc. A Waning Moon can be great for eliminating, exorcising, releasing, letting go, deep cleaning, etc. You may also want to be mindful of the direction you are working in. Walk through your home clockwise to increase and counterclockwise to decrease. Magical practitioners may want to also consult planetary correspondences prior to doing this work, to include the energies of the proper day and hour. I myself also use these correspondences depending upon the outcome I'm desiring. I highly recommend planetary correspondence apps, of which there are a few, to make this super easy to look up and apply. If you really want to get deeper with this, work with the elementals and directions, find out what elements correspond to North, South, East, West if you wish to incorporate them into your work, and start your process facing that direction. These may change depending upon your tradition. North is usually Earth, West is usually Water, but South and East may swap the elements of Air and Fire.

For example, if you are wishing to bring luck and prosperity into your home, consider using an herb or blend specifically designed to bring this vibration to you. Use the energies of Jupiter which include wealth, luck, prosperity, joy, success, fortune, abundance, etc. You may want to do this on a Thursday (a Jupiter day), during a Jupiter hour, during a Waxing Moon while visualizing yourself happy and joyful, surrounded by wealth and success (whatever this means to you), to make this ritual extra special and full of prosperity energy! Perhaps you may need some extra help eliminating illness, trauma, arguments, or chaos from your home to calm and soothe. You may want to do a cleansing during a Moon hour, during a Waning Moon, with the intentions of clearing these emotions away, and then on a New Moon with some sweet herbs to heal emotion such as lavender, sage, or sweetgrass, possibly on a Sunday. If you are using planetary hours in your work, consider that the hour may be more important than the day, if you can't work on the specific day you need to. These things really do work well, regardless of your spiritual leanings, or lack thereof. As always, you can do any smudging at any time for any reason. If all of the above seems daunting to you, take what works and eliminate the rest. The only rules that really matter are your own!

If you are doing other ritual observances, you may wish to include this as part of the larger ritual. Clean and declutter your home as best you can. Take a soothing bath or shower, put on clean clothing. Place any jewelry or crystals on you that work for you to elevate the energies as you choose. Again, be careful of flowing clothes or hair, and dangling jewelry, to avoid fire hazards. Turn off any televisions or devices, eliminate as much noise as you can from your space. You may choose to play some healing music, or even some driving music that motivates you depending upon the goal of your ritual. Or, simply have as much quiet as you can, which is what I personally prefer. Have your smudging items at hand before you begin. Ground and center. Light your coal and place into your burner. As you are waiting, focus on your intentions for this smoke cleansing. Call in your Allies if needed, this includes your Higher Self, Guides, Deities, Land Spirits, Ancestors, etc. Relax into sensation awareness[9] as you center and feel into your body, energy field, and the home's energy. Find your starting point in your house or property as discussed previously. Drop fresh herbs and resins onto your coal, and walk in the direction you choose. Wave smoke into the room as you walk, speak your prayers or mantras if you have them. Keep your intentions for this ritual in your mind as you focus on the end result. Always speak to your home with love, tell it what you are doing and why. As stated previously, pay particular intention to corners, windows, doors, under furniture, etc. Scrape off burnt material and place fresh material onto the coal to keep the smoke fresh and vibrant. Move from room to room in this way, until you have made your way back to the start. Relax again into awareness and center. Bow and give thanks to your Allies and the house spirits. Now is the time to crack open a few windows to allow all the smoke you have created escape in each room. While doing this, visualize unwanted energy leaving. When you close them, you may want to visualize goodness, joy, love, light, etc. pouring in. Depending on the time of year, don't forget to shut them again to disallow your heat or air conditioning from escaping too. I can hear my Dad's voice now "shut the window, were you raised in a barn?!"

Blessing for the Spirits of the Home/Land

I believe homes have an energy of their own, a "House Spirit," if you will. There are many folk tales of house elves and gnomes, such as the Scandinavian Tomte, a Scots Brownie, or British Hob, amongst many others, that would always be left offerings to ensure a happy home. It was believed by many cultures, that if you dishonored or angered the house spirits, they may get up to all kinds of nasty business, including putting their occupants in real danger. No matter what you call the spirit of your home, honor it by leaving it offerings, including incense. This work can create harmony and balance, and great energy for you and your fellow housemates.

Find a day to do this regularly, perhaps on a New Moon. Be sure your home is clean before you start. Locate what you perceive to be the heart of your home and create an altar or offering place. For this ritual, this may be the kitchen or hearth/ fireplace in a center room (you do not need to have a hearth to do this, but if you do, having it lit is even better). Or, just use a small table, or other piece of furniture. Obtain herbs that may be a native to the area of the world in which you live. If you have pretty stones, wildflowers, feathers, leaves, snakeskins, bones etc. that you have found locally, place these on your altar. I have an arrowhead I found in my yard, cleansed it, thanked the Peoples of the Land who came before me, and placed it on the mantle of my fireplace, along with antlers, stones, and feathers. Fireplace mantles make fantastic mini altars. Place food and drink offerings on your altar or hearth. You usually can't go wrong with some fresh bread and cheese, fruit, some wine or beer, and water if you want to keep it simple. Depending on where you live, you may want to place something traditional for them, buttered porridge being common in Northern Europe. Jason Miller has a wonderful Spirit Feast ritual that I have adopted in my own practices, and is very rewarding![10]

Ground and center. Stand or sit in front of your offerings. Consciously connect with intention to the spirits of the house or the land upon which you dwell. Use sensation awareness to feel your body and the energy of the space. Light your incense and candles and hold your hands over your offerings to consecrate them with your energy. Find a chant or charm, or speak words of power, as you make your connection. Here is one I came up with you may enjoy:

O Spirits of my Home, Spirits of this Land, welcome all!
Please join me in my hallowed hall!
I give great thanks, I raise my cup
I honor you tonight, to feast and sup!
Bless this home with peace and joy
These gifts I offer, enjoy, enjoy!

Have your own cup and plate of food, leave the spirits their own. Sit with them and see if you can feel subtle energy shifts, and what your space feels like, sounds that occur, changes in light and shadow. When you feel you are ready to close the ritual, thank the Spirits for their presence, ask them to bless and protect you and your home, and bid them farewell. Close your ritual as you see fit. Blow out the candles, let the incense burn down. If you have a place to bury the offerings do so. Be careful of pets or small children getting into your offerings, and place them up high until you can dispose of them. You can make this ritual as short or long as need be, depending on how regularly you do this.

Chakra Cleansing Ritual

Remember you have more than seven chakra centers in your body. This would be a pleasant and empowering ritual for you to cleanse and balance these energy centers, and will make you feel wonderful afterward! This ritual involves vocal toning through seven chakras, but you may also skip this if you wish. You will not be singing, so it truly doesn't matter if you have any kind of vocal ability. This exercise can also balance you and is great for a vagus nerve reset.[11] Vocally tone each chakra three times before moving up to the next one. Do this loudly, vibrate the walls if you can! If you are color blind or have aphantasia, remember to just do this any way that works for you. You can also do this exercise sitting down if you have mobility issues. This is basic chakra work, I will not go into too much detail about the function of them, there is far more information that you can take a deep dive into regarding this topic. You can find a great resource about chakra toning from Jonathan Goldman.[12]

Ground and center. Relax in quiet or with some soothing ambient music. Become aware of the energy of your current space, to be grounded and fully present, to feel how your physical body feels in this moment, and be aware of how your surroundings feel. Light your coal or herb bundle. As you are cleansing each chakra point visualize it in whatever way it comes to you. See it pulsing or spinning, and see the color if you can. Starting at your feet, if you can, run your feet through the smoke to cleanse these centers. What color do they look like to you?

You can also visualize the colors layering over your body in order like a rainbow as you move up (red on the inside, violet on the outside) and cover the outside of it all when finished with a layer of chrome or mirror if you need some extra protection for this day for any reason.

Move up to the Root Chakra, Muladhara. Smudge this area at the base of your spine by wafting smoke between your legs, around your buttocks, etc. Visualize ruby red in this area, and chant at the lower register of your voice, the sound UHHHH.

Next is the Sacral Chakra, Svadhishthana. Swirl smoke around your lower belly, and lower back. Visualize a beautiful, bright orange. At a little higher tone, chant the sound OOOO.

Next is the Solar Plexus Chakra, Manipura. Smoke the upper belly/diaphragm area at your ribs and around your back.

Visualize a bright, sunny yellow. At a little higher tone, chant the sound OHHHH.

Move up now to your Heart Chakra, Anahata. Smudge your chest and around your upper back. Visualize emerald green (you can also "see" pink with this, this is thought to be the color of the "high heart" between the heart and throat). Raise the tone in your voice higher to chant AAAAHHH.

Next is the Throat Chakra, Vishuddha. Waft smoke at your throat and around your neck, and the base of your head. Visualize an azure blue/turquoise blue, the color of a deep blue sky. Raise your vocal tone again and chant AYEEEEE (pronounced "eye").

Next up is the Third Eye Chakra, Ajna. Bring the smoke to your forehead and waft around your head. Visualize a deep midnight blue. Raise the tone to chant AAA (pronounced just like the letter "a").

Lastly we have the Crown Chakra, Sahasrara. Raise up your smoke to the very top of your head. Visualize a beautiful violet purple. Raise the tone to the top of your vocal register and chant EEEEEE (pronounced just like the letter "e").

If you have it in you to go up again higher still, visualize the Soul Star Chakra above your head in glittery white (I call it the Wiracocha as previously discussed). Hum/chant loudly the tone MMMMM with your teeth and mouth closed. This creates a nice vibration in your head, and feels amazing!

When finished, you may want to re-ground yourself by chanting in a downward register back down through the chakras to the feet again, re-center yourself and relax for a few minutes. Drink some water and be sure you are well grounded before you get back up again to continue with your day. This may be more easily done for some with an herb bundle or Palo Santo stick, but regardless, be sure to be careful of loose embers. There are variations of this ritual and this can also be done with crystal points or crystal wands if you use them, make it your own.

I teach a variation of this in my Reiki classes, an exercise I found from Alberto Villoldo, PhD, of the Four Winds Society.[13] It is a chakra-cleansing ritual to do in the shower, much the same as above. I decided to add the vocal tones to it whilst doing it, and adding sparkly light and the Reiki symbols to the water. This involves rotating your dominant hand counter-clockwise on each chakra, while visualizing the colors and toning, and grabbing and pulling out stale energy, washing your hands off in the stream of water, then repeating this on the next chakra. Once you have made it to the crown, start over again at the root and do the exact same thing, except rotate your hand clockwise to spin them properly again. I can honestly tell you, the reason I teach this method of energy clearing is because it works so amazingly well! I feel energized and my attitude definitely improved when I have done this. I try to do this weekly if possible.

Smoke Scrying

Scrying, the art of seeing spirits or visions in crystal balls and special mirrors, is an art anyone can try. You can use anything for a session which includes, of course, crystal spheres, but also incense smoke, candle smoke, flames, bowls of water, pools and puddles in nature, mirrors of all kinds, or anything with a reflective surface. This is an art that requires quite a bit of regular practice. To do divination in clouds of smoke (capnomancy) is to be able to see patterns in the smoke and decipher them, much like you would reading tea leaves (tasseomancy).

Ground and center. Find a space in which you can focus on the smoke clearly, possibly with a plain solid color background. Quiet your mind and relax or meditate in whatever way works best for you to alter your consciousness slightly. Light your coal and let it ash over and drop your herb/resin of choice onto the coal. Tell the herb what it is you need. Gaze into the smoke and try to see patterns, or even images. You do not need to have a specific issue or question in your mind, just notice what you notice. If you do have one, use your intentions to concentrate and focus on this question. Let things come to you in their way, and it is possible something may come to you later as you dream. Be sure to write down insights and images afterward, and be open to signs and answers later. If you like charms, this is one that came to me:

Smoke I see, it sees me, visions and insight come to me

Chapter 4

Wildharvesting

Seek wisdom in books, rare manuscripts, and cryptic poems if you will, but seek it out also in simple stones, and fragile herbs, and in the cries of wild birds. Listen to the whisperings of the wind and the roar of water if you would discover magic, for it is here that the old secrets are preserved.

~ Scott Cunningham

Collecting herbs for smudging or other uses in the wild is a fantastic way to get yourself out into nature, especially since many of us don't get outside time nearly enough. Any time you are spending with wildlife in the fresh air and sunshine is always a healthy pursuit for mind, body, and spirit. When outside, in your yard, the desert, or wild forests, take time to give thanks for the beauty that surrounds you. Take off your shoes if at all possible and ground to earth, not just to connect, but also to take in the natural ions and beneficial microbes that the bare earth gives back to you. It is scientifically proven to be of benefit to your overall physical health and well-being.

The first thing that should be stated if you have the notion to collect wild plants is to always be aware of who's land you are traipsing around on, and to have respect for the land itself. Be sure that these are public lands, or owned by someone from whom you have asked permission. If these lands are protected wildlife habitat, please do not harvest there, they are protected for a reason. Be sure there are not any posted signs, No Trespassing signs or otherwise. There can be hefty fines (or worse if you come across a particularly angry person) for trespassing, not to mention annoyance from friends or neighbors if you had not cleared it with them first.

It's always recommended to stay away from harvesting on roadsides, even if you see plants you need there. These plants can be corrupted with gasoline, oil, trash, or other chemicals such as herbicides and pesticides sprayed by state workers or homeowners. Keep clear of most farmlands for the same reason, as most of these nowadays use toxic chemicals that end up in the ground that your wild plants are growing. Do not harvest near or under power lines, because these emit harmful electromagnetic frequencies (EMF's) that may possibly affect the health of the plants near them. Harvest in an area that you are fairly certain has remained uncorrupted by pollution of any kind. If at any time you are uncertain about any of the above, there is a wealth of sustainably harvested and organic herbs available on the internet, and in many spiritual and metaphysical shops, as well as supermarkets that sell organic food-grade herbs with which you may want to smudge, including cooking sage, rosemary, and lavender.

Some plant collectors do not do so in the proper ways, and end up killing the plant, thereby thinning the population of in the wild and contributing to the problem. Be sure to only take around 20% to 30% of a plant, as well as the overall patch of plants. Move around and harvest a little from multiple patches. Never dig the plants if you don't have to, unless you are harvesting roots, but be sure once again, to leave other nearby plants intact. It is honorable to leave plants for others to be able to use, including the animals that may need them.

Many of us may not be able to see or feel them, but elemental beings and nature spirits are very real. To people in the Western world, this may seem odd, as many of us are not taught that there is anything other than what our five physical senses can use. Our world has strayed very, very far from the natural world, which is unfortunate. When we were children, we inherently knew these things, and could sense them, whether you remember or not. However, by the time we are fully immersed in formal education, indoctrinated into religion, and by junk food and technology, we have lost some of these abilities. If you remain still and have the highest intentions, you may be able to sense them if you tell them you wish to. You may even get a sign from them that they are around. Keep practicing this if this is something you wish to learn again, and it will come back to you in time. Feel the space around you as you walk, see if you can tell if the energy there feels, light, happy, or positive, which means you are welcomed in that space. If you feel "off" or in any way unwanted or creeped out, this is a very clear sign that you are not welcome in this space, and you may not want to continue searching for items to bring home. Any time you harvest anything from the land, do so with clear and honorable intentions. When you find the plants (or other items such as stones, feathers, crystals, etc.) you are looking for, always ask permission from the plants, and honor them and the earth elementals by leaving an offering. This can be anything from coins, water, natural tobacco (a traditional offering, but do not use cigarette tobacco because of the added chemicals), cornmeal, or other smudging herbs. Always say thank you aloud and give gratitude. Anything less can result in negative energy not just attached to you, but attached to the plants you harvested or the other items you have carried home. There is no need to conduct complicated rituals regarding this practice unless it resonates with you to do so, keep it simple so that you are always prepared and not frustrated by the process.

If you happen to follow almanacs, or plant and harvest by the Moon phases, Moon signs, and planetary day/hour currents as I do, there is specific information out there in other books and the internet, of course, and I encourage you to look into it. Many modern farmers and gardeners still use these methods, just like our ancestors always did. For example, general guidelines will include harvesting above-ground or aerial parts of plants during Waxing Moon phases (New Moon to Full Moon) and harvesting root crops during waning Moon phases (Full Moon to New Moon). However, there are also guidelines on harvesting during specific phases and signs the Moon happens to be in on any given day which makes things a bit more complicated. There are other reasons to prepare your herbs during certain Moon phases or planetary currents relating to the days and hours, depending upon what they are specifically being used for. There is far too much information on this topic to address here, and there are other resources for this purpose. I do recommend *Blum's Almanac*, and the advice of herbalists such as Rosemary Gladstar, among many others, as they are a wealth of information. I have had great success in using these methods in my own garden and spiritual practices.

Many of you do not live in areas where you are able to grow or wild harvest plants, and that is perfectly okay. Some plants, like California white sage or Palo Santo, for example, cannot be grown in most places in the world, and I never recommend wild harvesting white sage even if you live in an area in which it grows, unless you have grown it yourself on your own property. Sometimes, the best products are ones you can find in shops locally, or in many good quality online shops. You have every right to ask where their herbs are sourced from, if they know. For the most part, every shop (including mine), whether brick and mortar or online, who sells herbs of any kind, sources them from wholesalers who themselves purchase from sustainable herb farms. California white sage (Salvia apiana) specifically, is mostly sourced from sustainable sage farms in the southwest US. I used to buy directly from one of these farms, but they started selling to specific larger wholesalers, from whom I buy since I know the source. For this reason, you should have no qualms about purchasing this herb, or any other, from most reputable online shops, as the Trade is supplied worldwide from these sources, including edible herbs for cooking, and we can order much of our needs on the internet. White sage is an herb that is endangered in the wild not just due to over harvesting but also habitat loss due to development. Sage farms and their caretakers have helped this plant rebound and thrive, and have created a way for many people worldwide to enjoy this beautiful and healing herb.

A Word of Caution: Always know what your plants look, feel, and smell like. Never harvest any plant unless you are absolutely certain that it is your desired one. Many plants look similar to others, and there are plants that are very poisonous, and can cause serious illness. If in doubt, leave it! Know your surroundings and watch very closely for things like poison ivy, ground wasps such as yellow jackets, fire ants, snakes, etc.

Chapter 5

Making a Smudge Stick

He who works with his hands is a Laborer. He who works with his hands and his head is a Craftsman. He who works with his hands, and his head, and his heart is an Artist.

~ St. Francis of Assisi

If you have been smudging for a while or enjoy crafting, you may decide to make your own herb bundles. It can be rewarding, as well as a bit less expensive than purchasing them. This is easy to do, as well as enjoyable, and you may decide you wish to gift them to others. Use whatever burnable herbs your heart desires (as long as they are safe to burn), but the herbs must be somewhat fresh and free of pesticides and chemicals. Many of us do not live in areas where white sage grows and can be legally harvested, so this one may not be an option for you. If you live in an area that you can have a garden, you can grow many herbs yourself, and can pick them and bundle them when they are fresh. If you do not, but still wish to do this satisfying craft, see if a friend or someone at a local market has some fresh herbs you may purchase. Feel free to bundle together more than one herb, for example, sage and rosemary, rosemary and lavender, mugwort and cedar, or sage and sweetgrass, or any combination of multiple herbs. Experiment and see what works for you! Common plants for bundling include various sages, rosemary, lavender, junipers/cedars or other evergreens such as pine, thyme, mugwort (Artemisia), meadowsweet, and any combination of these.

I always recommend gathering your thoughts and making sure you are in a good frame of mind before bundling, just as you would when wild harvesting. Place your prayers and intentions in your thoughts while you create. Pick up a spool of cotton or other natural fiber thread and your stems of herbs, many people use sacred numbers like seven or nine stems. Make the stem ends even with each other and grab tightly at the end. Start winding the string around the end two or three times, then knot the thread. Start winding more thread, once again if sacred numbers resonate with you, wrap as many times as you need to. Seven is usually sufficient. Start wrapping up the bundle in a zigzag fashion, then back down again. Some do this step twice. Please be sure to wind the string as tightly as possible, as the herbs will shrink as the bundles dry, and you don't want them to be too loose when ready to use. When back up at the top again, tie another knot and voilà, well done! Hang your bundles upside down in a dry place, but not near any air vents. You will need to dry your bundle for a couple of weeks at least, depending upon your climate or time of year. Keep the bundle out of the direct sun, as it may fade and turn brown. You may want to consider hanging a brown paper sack over the bundle to keep out light and catch any falling herbs, as well.

Be sure to trim the ends neatly when finished to avoid flaming chunks of herbs falling off upon lighting. Be careful when burning your own handmade bundles, just as you would when using a purchased one. Some handmade bundles aren't as tightly tied or shrink a bit during drying, which could create extra air in the bundle and faster and hotter burning.

Chapter 6

The Herbs

I smile like a flower. Not only with my lips, but with my whole being

~ Rumi

Common Smudging Herbs

This chapter highlights the more common herbal burnables you will find at some point in your smudging journey. There is much more available to you than just white sage. Most of these are fairly easy to obtain, but be sure they are sustainably harvested. Some you may be able to grow in your own garden. Experiment with and enjoy all of them, you will find your very own favorite herbs and woods to use in your smudging practice. This is by no means an exhaustive list, there are many plants, especially for magical practitioners, that aren't listed here. There are other books to consult if you are needing a more extensive list with correspondences for your spiritual practices. Certain herbs may not smell the same when burnt as when fresh or dried, you may want to pair these with other herbs, but know that ritual blends aren't necessarily required to smell nice and are used more for their properties. If you choose to burn any herb in your censer, do your homework on the herb, be sure it is non-toxic and safe, as well as grown organically if at all possible. Not all herbs are suitable for burning.

A nice way to connect with your herbs when you obtain them, regardless of the means, is to speak to them, feel their energy, give them some of yours. Rub your hands together to raise energy. Hold them in your hands, or place your hands over them. Say hello to the plant spirit and ask it to be an ally and a friend. Tell it what you need from it, or just simply that you appreciate it and its energy. If you are adding it to a blend of other herbs, keep the flow of energy going as you mix with your hands. If you like to chant or speak charms, you may want to try a simple one such as this:

Herbal blend, be my friend. My energy to you I send. Do your work as I intend.

White Sage – *Salvia apiana*

White sage is a powerful healing herb...mixed with other herbs, the combination is heavenly. Bees love this plant and use it as a nectar source when in bloom, hence the species name "apiana". White Sage, or California White Sage, is native to the southwestern United States and northwest Mexico. It grows in dry desert-like environments and loves the sun and well-drained soil on the edges of the desert and on dry slopes. This plant only grows in USDA zones 8-11, and is not easily grown in other climates or soils. If, however, you are lucky enough to live in such a zone, give it a try and place some in your sunny, well-drained garden and harvest your own.

White sage is a sacred plant to indigenous Native Americans. Indigenous peoples of the tribes of the Desert Southwest consider it to be one of their most powerful medicinal plants, as are all sages (salvias). As with all smudging herbs, treat this plant with respect, it is not burned for incense or room freshening purposes.

Energetic properties of white sage are well known to be banishing of low vibration energies, clearing, calming, protective, blessing, and uplifting. White sage has the compound militrone, which has a mild sedative effect, and is a wonderful helper in soothing anxieties and calming nerves. The smoke can work by attaching itself to heavy energies and will carry it away and release it. Sage can burn as long or strong as needed, and the plant really does seem to know how much of it you need. In other words, the amount of smoke it produces can depend upon the amount of stagnant or heavy energy in the space.

There are a few ways to burn white sage, loose on charcoal tabs, or in a "wand" or "bundle" form of which may be very familiar to many of you. If burning loose, scrape away the burnt bits of sage after a couple minutes and reload the charcoal with fresh leaves, to avoid too much of the scent of burnt material.

White sage is to the point of being overharvested, so if you do purchase some, feel free to ask if the supplier is a sustainable source. Many suppliers have their own sage farms, plant sage regularly, and know how to harvest so as not to harm the plant and allow the plant to continue growing and recover from cutting. If you live in an area where wild sage is growing, please only harvest a little bit from the tops of the plant, only harvest a small bit of a grouping of plants, no more than 25% to 30%, and be sure to leave others completely intact. It is preferable at this time to simply just not wild harvest white sage at all, and purchase it from sustainable sources that buy from sage farms. Contrary to some information, much sage is grown well in large farms in the desert southwest, and large and well-respected herb shops online have posted about the farms they purchase from. This plant should be able to remain growing in the wild without human intervention. Please do not buy sage from someone who says it is "wildharvested," unless you know for a fact this person grew it on their own land for this purpose.

Note: This herb has been particularly contentious, due to its rarity in the natural world at large, overharvesting and loss of habitat, and because of its sacredness in indigenous North American tribes' ceremony. I am a white American person of European descent and I will never speak over the voices of indigenous people. Please seek out these peoples if needed to help clarify your feelings about using this plant. "Smudging" as stated in the beginning of this book, is a word of Germanic origin. Smudging is not a "closed practice" nor is sage (sage is a plant, not a practice). What are closed practices, however, are Native American spiritual practices such as Smudging Ceremony, certain dances, and special clothing and regalia. "Smudging Ceremony" is considered to be a closed practice, "smoke cleansing," which is what this book is about, is not. Please be honorable in your own practices, do not appropriate ceremony from cultures that you are not a part of, or from practices that are closed to those not of a specific tribe or culture, and obtain this plant and all others, from sustainable sources.

Cedar or Juniper – *Juniperus or Cedrus spp.*

Cedars and junipers can be used interchangeably, and constitute a few different types of trees. What many of us call fragrant cedar, which is used in closet lining, cedar chests, and pet bedding, with the prickly foliage comes from the Eastern Red Cedar, which is in the juniper family, *Juniperus virginianus*. Western cedars, flat leaf cedars are from the Arborvitae (*Thuja*) family. Then, of course, you have the true cedars (*Cedrus*) like Atlas cedar or Himalayan cedar. Some sell incense cedar (*Calocedrus* or *Libocedrus*). Most cedar you purchase for smudging purposes will be the flat cedar leaves, either loose or bundled. We live in the southeast U.S., and we wild harvest juniper leaves and berries (Eastern Red Cedar) and use some of the shavings as well. Any of these are generally regarded as suitable for smudging, I also use juniper berries in a couple of my own blends.

Most Native American traditions consider cedar to be a sacred medicine plant regarded as old and wise, and is handled with great respect. Cedar boughs are laid on the ground in traditional sweat lodges, and bits of cedar are used in medicine bundles and pouches. Burning cedar in your smudging rituals is a welcome addition, and can be very grounding, as well as a powerful clearing, protective, and blessing plant. Cedar should always be used in some fashion when doing a house blessing, especially when moving into a new home. Mix tobacco with cedar to gain the attention of spirits that you have invoked. Cedar mixes well with most smudging herbs and is very popular for the healing properties, as well as the scent. For medicinal use, cedars are infection fighters and true healing plants. Juniper berries are used in foods and beverages and have been for thousands of years by indigenous peoples all over the world.

There are certain areas that these plants are protected. If you wild harvest any tree material at all including cedars, use sterile and sharp clippers and cut above the little "collar" that the twigs create at the bottom. Only cut a little bit from each tree and be aware that a woody plant such as this can be slow growing and may not recover from too much pruning and damage.

Tobacco – *Nicotiana spp. or Lobelia inflata*

One of the four sacred medicines of the Native Americans, tobacco is used when harvesting plants as an offering plant for Spirit and the nature elementals, offering to tribal elders, in medicine pouches, to bless ceremonial drums and implements and create sacred space. In sacred pipes, it is not inhaled. It is said to be a plant that facilitates spirit communication, absorbs negative energy, and attracts blessings. Tobacco juice is ingested in some shamanic training systems to induce visions (don't try this at home!) This plant is also used in many spiritual paths, including neo-paganism. In magical pursuits, tobacco is used as a substitute for datura or nightshade. Some will use this plant to sprinkle in the herbal mix when making your loose blends.

The nicotiana species of tobacco is imported, although this is the tobacco most of us use and are familiar with today. However, Indian Tobacco, traditional and native to the Americas, is a completely different plant. Its botanical name is Lobelia inflata. This plant is grown by some Native Americans to this day and is used in their sacred smoking blend called kinnikinnick, along with bearberry and red willow. Lobelia inflata is a plant well known for its medicinal properties by herbalists and wise women.

If using Nicotiana, purchase raw leaf organic tobacco. Do not harvest from tobacco fields, as this is sprayed with many chemicals. Do not use tobacco from cigarettes for the same reason. Natural tobacco is worth purchasing to have on hand to use not only in your smudge bowl, but sprinkled by plants and trees as an offering to the elementals. Tobacco is, of course, considered to be a toxic plant, so use sparingly. This is another plant that can be used as a local plant spirit in places that it is commonly grown, such as the Southeastern U.S., which is where I live. I am surrounded by tobacco farms, some of which are also organic farms. The local spirits of place are familiar with this plant and the people who farm it and use it, so I use it sometimes for offerings to them along with other materials and water.

Tobacco, either wild or cultivated, is a very powerful medicine plant regardless of your spiritual path, and must be handled and treated with the utmost respect.

Sweetgrass – *Hierochloe odorata*

Sweetgrass can also be called buffalo grass, and is another of the Four Sacred medicines in Native American culture. It is considered to be the sacred hair of Mother Earth. You will usually see it in a long braid, which represents honesty, love, and kindness or body, mind, spirit. It is woven into ceremonial regalia, as well as into beautiful baskets. Those of you that know this plant also know why it is one of the most popular smudging plants. It is one of my favorite plants to use in the smoke bowl, and is a part of our handmade blend. It is a healing plant with calming effects and positive vibrations. People will light the tip of the braid after using other smudging herbs, to attract benevolent spirits and good, soothing, happy energy, after the clearing of negative energy. It is also wonderful to burn sweetgrass before any sacred ceremony.

Sweetgrass grows throughout the world. Is used in European cultures as well, as a strewing herb and to sweeten foods and beverages, including candies and teas. This beautifully scented grass is also sacred in Scandinavian culture, and braiding sweetgrass is common in Northern Europe, as well as here in the U.S. In the Americas, sweetgrass is becoming endangered because of the trade. If overharvested in a non-sustainable way, the damage could be irreparable. If you harvest for yourself, please DO NOT pull out by the roots. Only cut the plant at the proper time for harvesting, which is mid-summer through fall, and only if the plant is growing in a large enough patch to sustain it. You can try to grow this grass fairly easily in your own garden, provided you have a fairly well-drained, but moist area in the sun. Heavy clay and rich soils are not recommended for growing sweetgrass. It can grow quite easily and take over, so plant in a place where you allow it to do what it wants, and subsequently, have plenty of it to harvest.

Desert Sage & Silver Sage – *Salvia spp. or Artemisia spp.*

There is great confusion in the community as to what these plants are, and their names are sometimes used interchangeably. Some artemisias are also called sage (see the Mugwort entry for more details on this specific plant). It is important to know what you are buying, harvesting, and burning, especially if you are a stickler for specific plant properties. Many sellers don't even know the plant they are selling and call everything sage. Desert sage, purple sage, Texas sage, sometimes called sagebrush, are the same plant, Salvia dornii, and are in the Salvia family along with the ever popular white sage. True silver sage, Salvia argentea, is a wooly larger-leaved sage native to Europe. Different species of artemisia are also called silver sage, sagebrush, black sage, or desert sage, so you can see the problem here. You can tell the difference if you look up the images of these different plants. These have all been used for many purposes, including in poultices and teas. Do not ingest any plant unless you are a trained herbalist and know exactly which one you have in your possession.

Woody plants in the Artemisia family are used very commonly for smudging purposes, especially when white sage is not available. For the most part, when you see the words "silver sage" or "desert sage" this is going to be the plant that you are using. Artemisia varieties, also known as mugwort (Artemisia vulgaris) or wormwood (Artemisia absinthum), also have a heavenly smell, and this was the first smudge bundle that I had ever used, and was sold as Silver Sage. I was enamored of the effects and have been a proponent of smudging with artemisia ever since. As an aside, wormwood, along with other herbs including fennel, is used in the making of the alcoholic beverage known as absinthe, as well as vermouth. Do not use plants in the artemisia family lightly, these are powerful medicines. If you can find it to grow, I highly recommend Artemisia absinthum in a sunny garden spot, it is quite beautiful, an insect repellent, and smells absolutely divine. It can be a bit invasive, however. There are many different types of plants in the wormwood family, and some cultivars sold at nurseries and garden centers. They are great plants for any perennial garden, however, if you are growing them for medicine plants, it is recommended to use the non-hybrid varieties.

Regardless, these all have lovely clearing and blessing properties, so if you live in an area where one or more of these grow, and can harvest them sustainably, by all means do so. As a matter of fact, other varieties of sages in the past were used much more often than white sage, because of their widespread availability, as white sage only grows in certain areas. Any plant in the artemisia and salvia families can be used without qualm by everyone worldwide, are easily grown and obtained, and may be recognized by your local spirit friends. Every part of the world has members of the artemisia and salvia family indigenous to its area, as all of the sages are true plant helpers and healers for humankind.

Mugwort – *Artemisia vulgaris*

Mugwort is another well-known plant native to many areas of the world and is also a very special ally for me personally. This particular artemisia is separated from her sisters and deserves special attention. It is an herbaceous perennial, instead of woody and can be a bit invasive. It can be commonly seen growing on roadsides and ditches happy and carefree. It is used in the Native community in sweat lodges and burned beforehand. It is used in poultices, insect repellents, and for poison ivy, and is another amazing healer plant. Chinese acupuncture uses mugwort in moxibustion practices, with which you may be familiar if you have been to an acupuncturist. Mugwort is also known to love to grow at the homes of healers and witches. When I moved into the home in which I live at this present time, after a year or so a tiny clump of it seemed to appear out of nowhere next to the garden. I realized as it grew that it was mugwort! This is one of my plant allies and it just showed up for me. I let it grow in a giant patch (much to my husband's chagrin, because it creeps into everything), and harvest and use it constantly for myself and in the incense blends I make and sell.

Mugwort can be harvested and tied to hang over your bed, or woven into a dream catcher to induce dreams and visions, spirit contact, over doors for protection, and for divination purposes. Contrary to old fear-based propaganda, it attracts (not repels) the Fair Folk for those who are connected to the Fayerie realm or follow the Fayerie Faith, and I and others I know, use this herb regularly for offerings. It can be used as a tonic, a tea for digestion, sleep, and women's issues such as menopause support, and to flavor food by some who know the proper dosages. Mugwort can have mild sedative and mind-altering properties. This particular artemisia deserves a word of caution. Use particular caution when burning this powerful herb, always have proper ventilation, and never, never, never burn it around, or feed it to, pregnant women, small children, and small pets. I know someone personally who had a pet bird die because someone was burning mugwort near its cage, and this was the suspected cause of death for the poor thing.

If you or anyone near you is pregnant or planning to become so, do not burn mugwort in their vicinity. This plant has been known to cause miscarriage and bleeding, and induce labor. It is considered to be an abortifacient and emmenagogue.

Palo Santo – *Bursera graveolens*

The name palo santo literally means "Holy Wood." Palo santo is a tree which grows in the dry forests of South America, mainly Ecuador and northern Peru, as well as Central America. Bursera graveolens is a relative of the copal, frankincense, and myrrh trees. Palo santo is used traditionally by the healers of the indigenous peoples of Central and South America for medicine, purification, and ritual, but is so well loved for its sweet and beautiful scent, as well as its energetic properties, that is now used throughout the world. It is clearing, protective, and brings in uplifting and positive vibrations. It is also a favorite of ours! The majority of the harvesting of palo santo is sustainable and carefully monitored and protected so the tree does not become endangered. The wood is only harvested from older and naturally fallen wood, never cut, and is only used when the wood has aged on the ground for a minimum of four years up to ten years. It is said that this is when its healing properties are in full effect.

The palo santo tree is also being studied by Western science for its possible cancer fighting and pain relieving effects. It is also used for insect repellent, colds and allergies, migraines, and nausea. This plant can be used in many forms including lit sticks of the wood, powder or resin forms to be burnt on a charcoal tablet, as well as a healing essential oil in aromatherapy.

Since this tree is protected, purchasing it from a reputable source means you are contributing to conservation and sustainability of this plant. The majority of this wood that is sold comes from a family farm in South America that replants many of these trees. However, the demand has increased, and like white sage, unsustainable practices have escalated. Palo santo is another one of Mother Nature's greatest gifts of healing plants to humanity, Please burn with the utmost respect and honor.

Sage (common garden) – *Salvia officinalis*

Don't want to use white sage? Use easily obtainable, easily grown, and beloved worldwide Salvia officinalis, common garden sage. If you have a garden of any kind, you can grow this easy and beautiful herb mostly anywhere, it has gorgeous purple flower spikes and is perfect for perennial gardens. You can harvest it as much as you want, you can eat it, it smells amazing, and is completely sustainable. The word sage, of course, means "wise" or refers to a mystic or "Wise Person," and is perfect for using with spirits you wish to gain wisdom from, or as an offering to a "Wise One." It is, of course, no coincidence that I use the word "Sage" in the title of this book!

Garden sage has similar properties as white sage, without the potential problems of unsustainability or accusations of cultural appropriation. It smells a bit different, but still has a lovely and somewhat spicy herbal scent. Since it is grown worldwide and is a common plant in Europe, sometimes this and other salvias may help someone of European descent connect with their own culture during their meditative and spiritual practices, without feeling appropriative in any way. Sage can help you connect with divine wisdom and insights from your chosen deities and ancestors, as well as help you tap into your own inner wisdom as a direct connection to the all. It too will clear space, is used for physical, mental, and spiritual healing, memory, clarity, protection, and to invite uplifting and soothing energies into your field. Sage pairs well with just about every burnable herb, especially the ones you can cook with such as rosemary and thyme, and make a delicious blend.

Many people when writing about sage, blend common sage with white sage and conflate the two. Know that garden sage is perfectly acceptable and sustainable for any person to use for any reason. Garden sage should be burned a bit more sparingly due to its thujone content, but is for the most part safe, and obviously safe and delicious to use in food preparation. Salvia officinalis essential oil, however, can be a bit toxic, as it is highly concentrated and volatile. It is generally best to not use essential oils as burnables because of their highly concentrated nature.

Yerba Santa – *Eriodictyon californicum*

Yerba santa, also known as "Holy Herb," is a small aromatic evergreen shrub native to the west coast of the U.S. and northern Mexico. It has also been known as consumptive's weed, bear weed, and mountain balm. It is a fantastic plant for regenerating areas devastated by wildfire, and important to the region, as well as a food source plant for wildlife. Indigenous peoples of the western U.S., such as the Chumash and Shoshone people, have used this plant as a healer for allergy and respiratory issues, poultices for broken bones and wounds, and insect bites. It can be used in teas, as a digestive aid, and to mask the bitter taste of medicines.

Used in smudging and ceremony, yerba santa helps create sacred space and works as a healing plant not only for physical wellness, especially during and after illnesses of a respiratory nature, but also for psychic clearing and blessing, encouragement, courage, spiritual awareness, and protection of the sacred space within. Yerba santa's leathery leaves have a delicious sweet but balsamic herbal scent, and can be crushed and burned on a charcoal tablet. We use this wonderful plant in our Everyday Hearth & Home Smudge Blend, as it adds yet another healing component to a powerful medicinal mix.

Lavender – *Lavandula spp.*

Ahhh lovely lavender! No herb or incense book would be complete without the addition of this amazing plant, used as a burnable especially in blends such as our own Everyday Hearth & Home Smudge Blend. Lavender is native to Europe, especially in warmer and drier regions, such as the Mediterranean. Lavender can be grown in sunny gardens throughout the world (it does much better in dry and well-drained sites), and is one of my favorite additions to herb and perennial gardens. It is a woody plant, with lovely silvery blue-gray foliage and its trademark light purple flower stalks. There are many varieties of plants in the lavender family, all are wonderful to use for any reason. This amazing plant has been beloved worldwide throughout history. Such a versatile plant with applications far too numerous to mention here, lavender is a must-have in any household either in dried herb/flower form, or essential oil blend, and is fairly safe to use in any form.

The addition of lavender buds to an energetic smudge blend not only adds an extra pleasant aroma to the smoke, but is encouraged to use for multiple reasons. It is a soothing, calming herb used to bring down high energies, for a peaceful household, and can have a mild sedative and anti-anxiety effect, as those who use lavender essential oil can attest. It is fantastic in a sacred blend and for magical uses, and some use this herb for love drawing as well. Lavender is a wonderfully purifying, healing, and protective herb and I don't hesitate to use it at every opportunity!

Rosemary – *Rosemarinus officianalis*

Everyone is familiar with the fantastic healing herb, rosemary. Not only is it a delicious addition to your favorite foods, but the plant is used for its antimicrobial effects of the fresh herb as well as in essential oil blends for this purpose, and also works great as an addition to hair tonics and shampoos. The herb and the oil are also used in blends to help with mental clarity, alertness and focus, or to clear the mind, and is fantastic to sniff when this is needed, such as when studying to retain information, for memory and a sharp mind, and to combat tiredness and brain fog.

Rosemary grows in the same environment as lavender and other herbs love to grow, in sunny, warm, and well-drained gardens. Much like many heat-loving herbs, rosemary does not like rich and heavy soils. In warmer zones, it is a woody perennial and the larger varieties can be grown into hedges. It is sustainable, easy to grow, and easy to obtain worldwide. No garden should be complete without the addition of this magical and healing plant! Wise Folk and healers will sometimes grow rosemary by the "garden gate" or front door.

When burned as an incense, rosemary is a powerful energetic cleanser and purifier and is very uplifting. Not only does it help to rid spaces of excess low energy, but it is a highly protective herb. Place it on a charcoal to burn by itself to divine answers to questions and clear your mind. Add it to your blends to provide an extra boost to your energetic smudging practices. Rosemary is truly one of my favorite herbs of all time and is one of the most beloved herbs in history. It is so versatile, that many people consider this herb to be an all-purpose herb to be used in place of any, when other herbs cannot be obtained. I don't entirely agree with this statement, as herbs have specific properties that aren't always interchangeable, but it can be a fine addition to virtually any incense for many reasons. It is one of my favorite daily-use herbs and essential oils.

Rose – *Rosa spp.*

As Shakespeare said, "A rose by any other name would smell as sweet." According to some, the energy field of the rose is vibrationally higher than any other flower. Roses look and smell beautiful and are uplifting and healing just being in their vicinity. This beautiful yet thorny plant has been a perennial favorite throughout history and revered as the Queen Of The Flowers in art and music. Roses are connected to sacred feminine priestesshood, ancient Divine Feminine wisdom, and female deities. The energetic properties of roses are, of course, love drawing, aphrodisiac, heart opening, beauty, calming and soothing, and trauma healing, and as a nervine to combat stress and anxiety. Roses are also used in medicine, food, and skin care, and make an excellent skin and hair tonic. Rose hips (the swollen ovary that forms after the petals are gone) are used for jellies and as a skin-healing oil and are loaded with antioxidants and an excellent source of vitamin C. Roses are one of my most very favorite flowers and scents, bar none.

Use dried rose buds or crushed dried petals anytime and in combination with other soothing or uplifting herbs to create a beautifully-scented blend to waft around yourself and home, and envelop you in a sense of comfort and calm. If you feel the need for more self-love and care in your life, as we all do from time to time, use roses to infuse your energy field with this vibration. Use roses or rose incense blends in love-drawing rituals, and to infuse your home with the sweetness of love and life. Pair this plant with other gentle and soothing herbs or resins such as benzoin resin, sandalwood, and sweetgrass.

If you use roses in your incense blends, be doubly sure you obtain them from an organic source, as roses are attractive to pests and fungal diseases and are regularly commercially sprayed with chemicals. As previously stated, be aware of how your plants are grown before you burn or ingest them.

Chamomile – *Chamaemelum nobile or Matricaria chamomilla*

A beautiful and uplifting addition to incense blends is the flowers of this gorgeous and sunny plant. Chamomile has been used in teas and skin care for centuries, and can be easily grown in sunny gardens throughout the world.

Chamomile is a nervine known best for its soothing, calming, anti-anxiety properties. It is a great stress reliever and is wonderful for good sleep. Purification, happiness, serenity, and protection are some of its properties. It has connections to Divine Feminine energy and is soothing like a loving mother's gentle touch, and was referred to as "Mother's Best Friend." It is also associated with the sun. This herb pairs well with blends used for calming and joyful purposes. The sunny yellow disks of chamomile flowers when dried look lovely mixed with other herbs and leaves and add a spot of joy to anything they are mixed with. I like to pair chamomile with white sage and mugwort, and a bit of sweetgrass to facilitate dreaming and sound sleep, and for ancestor and spirit contact.

Chamomile is antiseptic and good for the digestion. Use in the home with other calming, grounding herbs and resins when you need a bit of peace and serenity when stressed. Burned in the evening can promote restful sleep and good dreams.

Lemon Balm – *Melissa officianalis*

Lemon Balm is such a wonderful herb I have included it below Chamomile due to its nervine properties. Its genus name Melissa (Greek for honeybee) speaks to just how much bees and pollinators love this beautiful plant. Just these two plants together make a soothing and delicious cup of tea, and when burned with intent in an incense blend, its properties are beautifully calming. Lemon balm is easy to grow worldwide, and since it is a member of the mint family, very safe to eat, drink, and whatever you use it for. It is also considered one of the magical and truly healing plants that belong in a witch's garden. It is an ancient herb, grown for centuries, and beloved by all. It is most definitely one of the easiest herbs to grow if you have the space for it. Since it is in the mint family, be sure to give it lots of room, it will take over. Or, grow in a large pot. Harvest liberally and often.

Lemon balm's properties are for calm, peace, stress relief, cleansing and uplifting, love and romance, anti-anxiety, prosperity, emotional healing, digestive, in love-drawing rituals and blends, in prosperity blends, and as a natural insect repellent. Think of what you would use a sunny, citrus-scented herb in a blend for, it has many uses. Lemon balm in a burnable incense blend may not have the scent it has in tea or food, but use it for its energetic properties.

I blend my own garden-grown lemon balm in my Dreamweaver blend, with chamomile, mugwort, lavender and other sweet and soothing herbs. I can't get enough of lemon balm!

Mint – *Mentha spp.*

Mints in the Mentha family of plants will be included here. I will give an overview of these plants, many of them can be interchangeable. However, there is more information to be found if you need specific species properties and correspondences. Generally, most people will use either spearmint or peppermint.

Who doesn't love mint? Mint is another plant so beloved in the world, it has been grown worldwide for many centuries, and has many healing benefits. Mints can be added to smudge/incense blends for their properties of soothing, cooling, calming, and focus. Also used for prosperity and physical healing blends, including for digestion. Mints are energizing and uplifting while also bringing calm, clarity, and focus. It is used to bring in Spirit Allies, money-drawing, brings joy, and raises vibrations.

Magical folk use mint for many purposes, including before divination and protection during ritual. This is another herb that may not give much scent when burned, so burn with other herbs and create a blend that suits the purpose you intend. Mints are wonderful dried and used for strewing herbs and also make a great insect repellent (see Chapter 2, 'Strewing Herbs').

Just like lemon balm, mints are prolific in the garden, but are so easily grown. Be sure to harvest all you want all the time!

Sandalwood – *Santalum spp.*

A small and parasitic flowering tree, Sandalwood is one of the most beloved and healing trees of all time. Throughout history, sandalwood has been used in incenses and as a base for incense sticks, as well as a base note in perfumery. It was used in ancient Egypt as an ingredient in embalming. Because this is a tree and not a fast-growing herbaceous perennial, this plant has also been endangered throughout the years, and can be very expensive. The Indian government regulates use of sandalwood for incense and essential oil making, and the factories that make the deliciously-scented East Indian sandalwood soap, one of my most favorite soaps! It is an incredibly skin-healing plant, chock full of anti-oxidants and vitamins.

As an incense, most are familiar with sandalwood incense sticks. I use sandalwood powder and chips in a couple of my blends, as it makes the most incredible heavenly smelling smoke, and a wonderful base for the herbs I blend it with. Sandalwood is associated with the root chakra, and just like many woody herbs, is very grounding, warming, and brings one back into the present with calm and ease, and to promote inner peace. Use in meditation or anytime you need to infuse your space with sweetness and healing in any way, and use it for inner and outer spiritual connection. It works well in any blend used for protection and healing, as well as with heart-opening blends and plants such as roses.

Because of unsustainable overharvesting practices, Sandalwood has been on the brink of extinction. It is now grown in Australia in sustainable ways, monitored by experts, and carefully harvested so that this amazing tree can continue to grow and be used into the future.

Another plant under the Sandalwood umbrella of plants is Red Sandalwood (Pterocarpus santalinus), but is a different tree. This plant makes a good base for incense and some use it interchangeably, but doesn't have the scent or properties genuine Santalum does when used for incense.

Cinnamon – *Cinnamomum verum*

For this purpose, we will be talking about both True Cinnamon and Cassia, as they can be used interchangeably. Cinnamon has been used and traded since ancient times, and was one of the most sought after exotic spices. This beloved spice has many uses in teas, as well as savory and sweet foods and delicacies. Its scent and flavor are so emotive, and color our memories of holidays and special events, and even simple and lovely childhood memories of cinnamon toast for breakfast. Cinnamon is considered by some to be a superfood full of antioxidants, warming, anti-inflammatory, and good for the heart and gut.

Cinnamon has so many uses as an energetic spice placed into incense and oil blends. Its properties include, but are not limited to: prosperity, luck, success, victory, money-drawing, protection, fiery passion and lust, physical and mental healing, personal power increase, warming and soothing, or for anytime you need a bit of extra "fire" in an intentional blend or a working. I really enjoy using cinnamon especially in Autumn, as it just seems to be the perfect addition to fall and winter mundane and magical fun. I use cinnamon chips in two of my favorite blends, one for a luck and success blend, and another in a fiery protection blend. It would also work very well for a blend designed for family and ancestor work.

Be careful with cinnamon, as it can be sensitizing, especially if you work with the essential oil (again, not recommended to burn). Use it sparingly in blends, including in burnables, a little goes a long way.

Mullein – *Verbascum thapsis*

Mullein is an easily recognizable biennial "weed" which grows easily in cleared fields and waste places, as well as cultivated land. It is native to Europe and Asia, but has become naturalized and endemic in the US. Many of you reading this book who live around rural environments know what this fun plant looks like. It's first year, it grows pretty rosettes of fuzzy, gray leaves that look like lamb's ears (Stachys). Its second year, it sends up tall stalks covered in tiny, sunny yellow flowers. Herbalists use these flowers to make healing oils such as earache oil remedy. The dried stalks can be dipped in wax or oil and used as torches, and some herbalists and witches make "hag candles" from these, covered in wax and herbs, for burning for ritual purposes. When mullein comes up in random places in my garden and yard, I always let it grow. If it sprouts up in the way in places I really don't want it, it is easily pulled out.

Mullein is best known for centuries for its dried leaves in teas and tisanes as a healer for respiratory issues and illness, inflammation, expectorant, and headache, among others. People can inhale mullein smoke for respiratory purposes as well, much like Yerba santa, even though this may seem counter-intuitive. It is a common ingredient in herbal smoking blends. If you use it in these ways, be sure to filter the leaves, as the fine hairs can cause irritation.

Mullein's energetic properties are varied, but can be used in healing blends of all kinds, in protective and cleansing blends, for dreamwork and divination, to ward off unwanted spirit activity, and in contact with Earth spirits and the Fayerie realm.

Mullein is a beautiful and friendly herb, that seems to want to work with humans in healing ways.

Bay – *Laurus nobilis*

Bay laurel, a most joyous herb so beloved and tasty in stews and soups, and one of the most valuable herbs in any herbalist's or witch's apothecary. Bay is a small tree/large evergreen shrub grown for millennia in temperate climates. It is another easy to grow sunny perennial for anyone who lives in USDA hardiness zone eight or above. Everyone who has seen ancient Greek or Roman imagery has seen the wreath of bay laurel on the heads of warriors and emperors as a sign of victory and nobility. Laurel wreaths are placed upon the heads of winners of contests and as a sign of social status or divinity. Laurel was given to doctors, and is the origin of the word "baccalaureate." Bay leaves are used extensively in witchcraft and folk magic, commonly with charms, prayers, and spells written on them then burned.

Use bay leaves in any blend that promotes luck, wealth, love, success, victory, happiness, joy, fun, as a creative boost, healing, etc. Use in love-drawing blends to denote your worthiness and specialness, and attract this vibration to you. Use bay leaves to petition your Spirit Allies to draw a specific wish or need to you.

Hyssop – *Hyssopus officinalis*

Hyssop has a long and storied career as one of the best healing herbs for many centuries. It can be grown easily in sunny places worldwide, and is a pollinator-friendly plant. This herb has been in constant use since ancient times, and is spoken of in the Bible as a great purifier. Hyssops are easily grown in most sunny gardens. Many healers and witches have this plant either in their garden or dried for regular use. Hyssop is a wonderful plant to use in many energetic blends for the purposes of purification, self-care and healing, cleansing, uncrossing and eliminating curses and hindrances, to facilitate spirit contact especially in necromantic applications, and to ward evil.

I use this herb in my special "Samhain" Autumn blend for its properties of speaking with the Ancestors, and I also use it in purifying baths with sea salt. It is sweet and lovely and a definite plant ally for everyone.

Eucalyptus – *Eucalyptus spp.*

Eucalyptus is a large family of trees native to Australia and Tasmania and endemic in other parts of the temperate world. It is known for its oil and as a respiratory aid, as well as in the floral and craft industries for its beautiful foliage. They are fast-growing trees and are able to be grown in USDA hardiness zone eight and above. They are adapted to regions that are prone to wildfire, however, they can spread wildfire as well because of the amount of oils in the plant which burn easily.

Eucalyptus leaves can be well-dried and burned, especially with other herbs, to elevate the energy around you as it is very soothing and uplifting, for purification, wound and pain healing, respiratory issues, alertness, clarity and focus, in blends designed for strength and cleansing when one needs to move on, "burn bridges," or bounce back from hardships and loss. This is another wonderful herb to use in place of white sage, and is very easy to find. Have no qualms about using this plant in any way, it grows around the world at this time, is easy to obtain, and non-problematic for use by anyone.

Oud/Aloeswood/Agarwood – *Aquilaria spp.*

Oud has been referred to as Wood Of The Gods. This ancient and beloved tree releases its scent when its heartwood is colonized by a mold. The plant then forms its resin to fight the infection. Another tree threatened by overuse since ancient times, this incense may be one of the most sought after and expensive in the world and is more expensive than gold. Oud is sometimes created purposefully, by injecting Aquilaria trees with the mold spores directly.

In today's world, Oud is sometimes used for third-eye opening, to connect with the divine, and any kind of cleansing and healing need. It is used as an aphrodisiac, an analgesic, a stress reducer, in meditation, harmony and calm in the home, to rid oneself of harmful influences and negative energy, protective, a woody base note for perfume, and is a powerful skin healer.

Oud is not an easily obtainable plant for incense making, and is so expensive to be cost prohibitive. If you decide to purchase some, there are sources online, but be sure these are sustainable and knowledgeable sources, and that you are getting what you pay for. If you are lucky enough to have some, it should be treated with respect. Like many ancient plants and fragrances, Oud was reserved for the elite and royalty. In Islam, Oud is sacred to the Prophet Mohammed, and is burned in religious ceremony to honor Him.

Chapter 7

The Resins

Until the daybreak and shadows flee away, I will get me to the mountain of myrrh and to the hill of frankincense.

~ The Song Of Solomon

Common Tree Resins

Tree resins are the plant's sap and are considered to be the "blood" of the plant. Resins hold powerful natural plant and spirit energies. They are different than essential oils and are meant to be used in different ways. The most common way to use resins is to place them on a burning piece of charcoal tablet allowing the aroma of the smoke to fill the space, releasing its energy and essence. Resins usually do not have much scent until they are heated, unlike herbs which will have some scent whether fresh, dried, or burned. They are also a key ingredient in making incense sticks and cones, combined with essential oils and finely ground woods, such as sandalwood. They can be used for their aromatic qualities alone, as an aid to holistic healing, and of course, in spiritual and religious rituals worldwide. We burn them alone, or in combination with one another and occasionally combine resins with our herbs in the smoke bowl, to contribute to and enhance the effects of the herbs.

Frankincense (Olibanum) – *Boswellia spp.*

Native to the Middle East and North Africa, frankincense was used for religious purposes probably since before recorded history. From the worshipping of the sun god Ra by the Egyptians, or the sun gods Apollo and Helios by the Greeks, and even being presented by Balthazar, one of the three wise men, as an offering to the infant Jesus, this resin incense has been used by humankind as a connection to spirit and as a physical and mental healer. It may be used for any type of spiritual ritual or to enhance meditations. Its scent is beautifully uplifting as well as soothing.

Frankincense is a well-known and loved resin in ancient times, as well as modern. In days of old, the highly perfumed resin of frankincense was as valuable as gold. Many of us are familiar with frankincense from the story of Jesus' birth, in that it was given as a gift along with myrrh resin. it is one of the resins burned today in churches, sometimes along with myrrh and benzoin resins, and you may already be familiar with its lovely scent. It is said that the plant spirits of this resin can facilitate connection to deities and to invoke the Divine. Frankincense is a truly wonderful resin when physical healing is needed, and is another well-known antimicrobial. Burn during any illness or infection, viral or bacterial. Burn in sickrooms and homes where a person has been ill, or simply to prevent illness from taking hold, and to prevent infection when exposed to the sick. in spiritual practice, frankincense creates a sacred atmosphere that enhances meditation, reduces stress and tension, and uplifts one spiritually. It has been continuously used for over 3,000 years in magical and religious ceremonies and can deepen any religious experience.

Myrrh – *Commiphora myrrha*

Myrrh (Commiphora myrrha) comes from a thorny shrub with small white flowers that is native to the Middle East, North Africa, and Northern India. It possesses a richly bitter scent. Prized for its intoxicating perfume, myrrh was seen as a magical substance that was capable of connecting heaven to earth. The Egyptians believed that the chunks of resin signified the tears of Horus, the falcon-headed sun god. Known as punt or phun, it was included in their Kyphi incense, burned at sunset as a thanks and offering to the sun god, Ra. The Egyptians also used it during funerals and in embalming rituals, as it was thought to accompany the soul on its journey to the spirit world and afterlife. The Hebrews drank wine flavored with myrrh prior to worship. Myrrh, along with frankincense, was one of the three gifts presented to Jesus at his birth. This beautiful resin has been used in spiritual practices for thousands of years.

Burning myrrh on a charcoal tablet and inhaled when ill can speed healing of the physical body, especially when burned with frankincense and used in visualization of good health and youth. Myrrh has been used medicinally for millennia and is well-known to be a fantastic skin soother, anti-inflammatory, pain reliever, insect repellent, mouth and tooth healer, and wound healer, and you may find this incredibly healing resin and essential oil in many natural oral and skincare products.

Inhaling the scent of the burning incense or crushed resin results in tranquility and calm, heightened awareness of subtle energies and your sacred space, and awakening. It is a great tool to use before prior to or during rituals and meditation, as it can balance the link between our chakras. Add myrrh resin to any burnable to increase the powers of the other herbs and resins, especially and classically paired with frankincense. Use to consecrate ritual tools and altars. Opoponax resin (Commiphora opoponax) is in the same family of plants and has much of the same properties as Myrrh, so does not warrant an additional entry for the purposes of this book.

Benzoin – *Styrax benzoin*

Benzoin resin comes from trees in the Styrax family, indigenous to Sumatra, and is safely used in perfumery and incense-making as a fixative, as well as a flavoring in food, candy, and drinks. It has a beautiful vanilla-like fragrance.

Benzoin, while fantastic to burn on its own, also blends beautifully with other herbs and resins and is quite often used in church incenses alongside frankincense and myrrh. Benzoin is typically used for purification, which is why it is listed here, as well as for prosperity and abundance. It is extremely soothing and grounding, but is also a great antidepressant, very earthy and sweet. It is used in ceremony to raise the vibration of the space, as well as smooth chaotic energies. Benzoin is also known to be great for respiratory issues, for congestion, and allergies, and works well with other healing herbs and resins such as yerba santa and frankincense, for these purposes. Its essential oil is used as a skin healer, and can be used blended in soothing salves and balms. It's delicious fragrance also lends itself well to blending with cinnamon, cloves, or orange, and has been used in love drawing blends and heart opening to promote generosity of spirit. I use it in a blend with rose buds and lavender for this purpose. Benzoin is one of the resins I keep beside my smudge bowl, and I use it often.

Copal – *Bursera microphylla*

Copal comes from the Bursera tree in the regions of southern Mexico. This tree is a relative of palo santo, myrrh, and frankincense. The resin is formed when the tree is cut and a thick, milky liquid seeps out. It is very dark in color, but changes as it dries. Copal can be a golden, black, or white resin whose smoke many people believe helps carry messages to the spirit world and obtain divine insights. The indigenous peoples of Central America hold copal as very sacred and have used it in ceremonies since pre-Colombian times. The name for copal is "pom" in the Mayan language. Especially sacred is the resin that comes from a tree that has been struck by lightning or "Thunder Beings," and in the Mayan creation story, *Popol Vuh,* it is described as a "seeing instrument."

Copal is personally one of my most favorite resins, and I use it regularly. It is incredibly uplifting and brings vibrations of joy and happiness. The smoke from copal when smudged over the body is thought to cure various illnesses, to protect oneself against sorcery, sickness, and misfortune, purification, protection, and to cleanse the body after contact with sick persons and corpses. Healers have been known to use copal as a diagnostic tool to detect illness and energy blockages. It may be used for clearing and clarifying the mind. Copal is very uplifting and is a great antidepressant. It is used often for raising the vibration of a space, especially to clear low vibration energies, darkness, and stagnant energy. It is fantastic to burn after arguments, illnesses, depression, when you have done clearing or banishing rituals, or any time the mood needs to be lightened a bit. For this reason, don't burn copal when you are relaxing or attempting to sleep, as it has an energizing effect. Another great plant used for millennia for healing skin and respiratory ailments, as well as a burnable. The dried resin, when burned, emits an odor akin to frankincense but with a lighter, citrusy tone. It's clean, crisp fragrance is ideal for use in self-purification rituals, clearing a space, or purifying ritual objects. It is such a wonderful resin, and makes me feel so amazing after burning, that it stays next to my smudge bowl for constant use. This is my go-to resin burnable!

Dragon's Blood – *Daemonorops or Dracaena draco, Croton spp.*
Related to a popular houseplant, the Dragon's Blood tree from which modern resins are harvested, which include the species Daemonorops, it grows in Southeast Asia, specifically Sumatra, although the resin has been collected from different plants throughout the world, hence the differing botanical names. It has been used for centuries for varnishes, incenses, and dyes, and also medicinally for gastrointestinal, respiratory, skin issues, and embalming. This is also the source for Dragon's Blood ink.

Dragon's Blood resin can be used alone to completely neutralize energies, and bring them back to a stable place. Burned by itself, it can be used to clear the energy in a space and return it to complete neutrality. Used along with a blend with another herb or burnable, Dragon's Blood will amplify the properties of its companions in the smoke bowl. For example, if one needed to bring to neutral very negative or low energy in a home after an argument or depressive episode, burn Dragon's Blood, then reload your coal with this resin alongside white sage and sweetgrass, or copal to uplift and bring in positive spirit. Conversely, if one has had a party and the vibrations are a bit chaotic, burn Dragon's Blood to return the energy to a calmer state, then burn again with a bit of sage, lavender, benzoin, or soothing frankincense. Used in neo-pagan religions to increase the potency of spells and other incenses for protection, love, banishing, and sexuality. It can also be used in hexes and an added ingredient in spell jars for this purpose. In African-American folk magic, Dragon's Blood is used in mojo hands for money or love drawing and as incense to cleanse a space of negative entities or influences. Has interesting smoke patterns and a sweet, pleasant aroma. Another one of my very favorite and versatile burnables!

Pinion Pine (Trementina) – *Pinus edulis*

Who doesn't love the scent of pine? A life-giving tree for humans and animals alike and one of the many sources of delicious pine nuts. Indigenous to the high desert areas of North America, trementina (piñon resin, trementina de piñon, piñon pine resin) is a traditional and sacred medicine commonly used by Native Americans and gathered in the spring when saps run. Pine pitch, including from the pinion, is used in healing salves, soaps, and balms. One of my favorite old-fashioned skin-healing soaps is pine tar soap. Pine needles are also used in teas (it is rich in vitamin C), strewing, or as a burnable in a ceremonial fire or sweat lodge.

Another fantastic all-purpose tree resin, pinion has been used to heal, to balance and clear energies, and for fertility, compassion and mental strength. It is wonderful as a restorative, warming, uplifting scent, especially when feeling tired or burnt out. Burn by itself, or combine with other incense resins for a meditative combination. It has a sweet, smooth aroma reminiscent of high desert evergreen forests and Yuletide, and smells exactly what you would expect pine pitch to smell like. There is really nothing like burning a small chunk of pine resin, the scent is just so evocative and beautiful.

Chapter 8

Smokeless Smudges

Music is the mediator between the spiritual and the sensual life.

~ Ludwig van Beethoven

No smudging book would be complete without touching upon alternative methods of energetic cleansing. Occasionally, there may be times when you are not able to burn your smudge stick, or light the coal for your burnables. Perhaps you may have guests arriving and don't want the air to be thick with smoke, especially if there are people with asthma or allergy issues. For example, one may want to clear the energy of their office space, the home of another, or the interior of their car, etc. In these instances, burning herbs may not be practical or recommended. There are alternatives to energy clearing that work, and you may find that you wish to try multiple means of clearing and raising vibration. It is fun to experiment with all of these from time to time, and also to give you and your home a quick or smokeless cleansing.

Smokeless Smudging Sprays

Sometimes also referred to as Florida Water in the magical community, this can be purchased in commonly known brands made with synthetic fragrance oils, or make your own out of genuine essential oils. Smokeless smudging sprays are becoming popular with the explosion of essential oil products on the market nowadays. Basically, it is a spray bottle full of water and essential oils, or hydrosols (the scented water left from steam distillation of essential oils). Many people use 100 proof grain alcohol such as vodka, which is also used in herbalist tinctures. These not only work well for simple and natural air freshening, but, with intent, can be used as an energetic space clearing tool. These sprays are typically a combination of delightfully scented oils which can have energetic properties, as well. Some people feel guided to include springs or leaves of the fresh smudging herbs in the bottle (i.e., a white sage leaf) or possibly a charged crystal such as a quartz point to amplify and bless the spray.

Some common energetically-cleansing blends include, but are not limited to, oils of sage, cedar, juniper, cypress, pine, lemon, cinnamon, rose, frankincense, myrrh, palo santo, lavender, rosemary, peppermint, etc. There are many more one can choose from, and it is fun to do some research on the spiritual and magical properties of certain essential oils. Please feel free to make your own smudging sprays, this is a fun pursuit and you will infuse the spray with your own energy while doing so! I do recommend blessing your bottle in whichever manner feels right for you, by stating your intentions for the spray, a favorite prayer, or reciting a mantra that is meaningful for you. Please see Chapter 3, *Powerful Prayers and Rewarding Rituals*, for more information on basic rituals, charms, and prayers that you can use while making oils, Florida waters and sprays, and using them just as you would herbal smoke.

A basic spray recipe for a 4 oz. (118 ml.) bottle may consist of distilled water, witch hazel, grain alcohol* (or a combination), a chunk of sea salt or Himalayan salt, and 30 to 40 drops total of your essential oils. If you choose, for example, frankincense oil, lavender oil, and lemon oil, you would use between 10 to 15 drops of each oil per 4 oz. bottle. Shake well before spraying to blend the oils with the medium, as this is a natural recipe and the oils may separate.

* Never use rubbing alcohol, or any other alcohol besides food-safe clear grain alcohol such as vodka or Everclear.

Himalayan Salt, Sea Salt

Many of us are now becoming familiar with salt as a clearing and cleansing mineral, not just for seasoning your food! Salt of all kinds is highly cleansing and can remove impurities, preserve foods, clear negative energy, and help detox your body. By salt, I mean either pink Himalayan salt, pure sea salt, or black salt, not refined table salt. Choose salt in its purest form for clearing or ritual work. Salts, when placed around the home, work to keep the vibration in a home on a continuous basis when one cannot smudge as often as one wishes.

We all may be familiar with using sea salt in a cleansing bath to detoxify your body, or as a foot soak. This works very well not just for physical cleansing, but cleansing your energy body as well. Some use salt in dishes, blessed and placed at entrances or exits, underneath beds, in cabinets, etc. It is also highly protective blessed and sprinkled at the entrance to your home, or around the foundation of a house to repel unwanted energies and keep those of low vibration from entering. Please remember if using salt outside, that it will make the soil barren and can kill plants, so use wisely, or do not use outside at all, especially in a garden area.

Pink Himalayan salt is quickly gaining popularity and is a favorite of ours in our home and our cooking. This lovely salt is great for your health (no, not all salt is bad for you!) and is loaded with minerals that your body may be lacking due to the highly processed nature of our food and depletion of our soils in these days and times. We cook with it daily and it tastes fantastic! However, for energetic cleansing purposes, use Himalayan salt as you would use the sea salt in the above paragraph, or an even better way to continue the high vibe in your home, salt lamps. Pink Himalayan salt comes from, you guessed it, the Himalayan region of the world. It is mined from very deep salt deposits that were formed millions of years ago and hardened when the primordial sea evaporated and the pressure of the mountains.

This salt is free from any pollution and impurities, due to its age and depth and is natural crystal salt. The purest Himalayan salt is mined from thousands of feet beneath the mountain range, and is the darkest in color.

Pink Himalayan salt lamps come in many shapes and a plethora of sizes, from the most diminutive candle holders to the large (and extremely heavy) floor models, and every size and shape in between. Salt lamps work with the warmth of the low watt bulbs (or candles) placed within, and infuse the air with negative ions, much as an electric air purifier does. The soft orangey glow of these lamps is reason enough to have at least one in the house, it really does add a warm and gentle beauty and lovely ambience to a room. If using in the home for continuous energy clearing, I recommend one salt lamp per room, or one large lamp for open spaces. We have a salt lamp in each and every room of our house, and sometimes will keep them turned on all day and night. For the best continuous clearing effects, keep the lamps turned on at all times. Some sleep with one turned down low, which is very protective during dreamtime. As an aside, I also use pink salt in bar form, wrapped in cloth, to place my cell phone on at night, and next to our computers, to hopefully counteract any negative effects of these electronic devices.

Musical Instruments

Another fantastic addition to your energetic arsenal is none other than music! Throughout the world, music and instruments such as bells, whistles, shamanic-style drums or rattles, gongs, and singing bowls are used for this very purpose, to clear stagnant energy and bless the space. Many people keep a small bell on an altar or in their sacred prayer space. You can use these instruments in the very same way to bring a higher vibration into the household. It is thought that sounds such as these not only make dark energies scatter, but attract light energies and benevolent spirits. I know some folks who suspect an entity in their home will walk throughout the home and bang on metal pots and pans to clear the energy as well, which does work in lieu of a more ear-pleasing instrument. However, to clear a space with a drum, rattle, singing bowl, or bell, for example, simply walk through your home in the same manner you would for a smoke smudging while playing the instrument. Keep the sounds as continuous as possible, and say prayers and blessings as you go, if you are guided to do so. Chanting and singing is a wonderful way to bring your voice into this important practice, and infuses the process with positive and personal energy.

Alternatively, I highly recommend ambient music be played in the home. Music such as you would find for meditation, energy healing, worship, etc., works beautifully. Some call this "New Age" music, although any beautiful music that you appreciate will suffice. Keep the television and other distractions turned off as much as possible, as these will continuously suck energy away from you and your home, and are increasingly being thought of as very low, and very negative energetically. It is hard to keep a light and fresh vibe in a home with blaring televisions on continuously. Occasionally, you may feel a bit "airy fairy" and ungrounded, and it can also be recommended to play a bit of heavier music such as rock, if one needs to "come back to earth."

Crystals

Many of you reading this book may be somewhat familiar with crystals and their properties, or are interested in learning more about these. I am not a crystal expert; however, I do have a cabinet with some wonderful specimens I have collected over the years. This is a large field of study, as there are so many rocks and minerals that are available today with a plethora of energetic attributes, that I cannot delve into here. Many stones and crystals vibrate at high frequencies, and are helpers to those who utilize them for their energetic and magical properties. Some crystals when properly charged can immediately raise the vibration in a home, or on your person when worn, especially with intent. Large specimens, such as a selenite or a clear quartz crystal, in the middle of a home can anchor light energy, and/or have a highly protective effect, and some use combinations of different stones in crystal grids for the purposes of clearing, protecting, healing, or for prosperity and abundance. One can also place stones at the four corners of the home, inside or outside, or make medicine bundles with stones and herbs, for protection and blessing. What I can tell you is the effects of having these beautiful creatures in our home is very rewarding, can be a bit addictive, and lead to collecting gorgeous (but expensive) specimens. Of note, some crystal harvesting practices have been shown to be very problematic. The way in which these are collected may impact their willingness and ability to be of service to you in the way you may intend. Clear and cleanse these, speak to them, and give them your energy. Please try to be sure of where your crystals originated from. There are many problems with collecting crystals ripped from the ground, including in some instances with child labor, unsustainably harvested, which is why I do not collect many crystals anymore.

Chapter 9

Incense Blends

"How could such sweet and wholesome hours be reckoned, but in herbs and flowers?"

~ Andrew Marvell

In this last chapter, I will give you a few recipe blends to get you started, if you are interested in creating them for yourself. I do highly encourage you to do what I did, and try lots of different combinations and create your own special blends. If you are just starting out with incense or smoke cleansing, do not feel you will need to outlay a lot of money on every herb, resin, and censer out there in the world today. You can place any burnable herb that resonates with you or your situation in a censer, and focus on that single herb to do the work you intend. It is also nice to obtain them and burn them singly if you aren't familiar with them just yet, as it is a great way to gauge how an individual burnable smells, looks, and makes you or your home feel. Once you have an idea of how these ingredients work individually, it may be easier for you to decide what to do with them. You may even decide that you dislike a certain burnable so you know what you do not want to use in the future. You do not need to create blends or use multiple herbs and resins on a coal to get the job done. The herbs and resins from the previous chapters are all wonderful and fairly easy to obtain, and I have personally used them all. I have some favorites and some less than favorites, but have had positive experiences with them all. They really do have individual properties, so I do encourage you to experiment with them and decide for yourself.

You can also use simple incense sticks and cones, as these are plentiful and easy to obtain. However, they may be created with inferior ingredients or synthetic fragrances, and may not have the properties you desire. Many times, these types of incense are great for scenting your home, but lack the energetic properties of natural and loose herbs and resins. Stick and cone incenses can be easily made by you, or you can find high quality brands that use natural ingredients and oils. Stick and cone incenses are lovely and I also use these from time to time, but we will not delve into these for the purposes of this book. Regardless, blending herbs and resins is light-hearted and fun, enjoy the process!

Why Make an Incense Blend?

Creating blends is fun, even if this means you add a couple different herbs individually to a hot coal in chunks each time. What you will need to decide if you wish to learn blending, is the purpose of your mix. What will it be used for? What herbs will you be using and how much of each herb will you include in the ratios of your special blends? There are no hard and fast rules, which makes this more fun. Experiment at will!

If you are creating blends for yourself in your own personal situations for clearing and cleansing, protection, love, prosperity, etc., you may want to consider the individual properties of herbs instead of the region of the world they are native to, with no correspondences or spirit involvement needed. As stated previously, these practices are for everyone, regardless of any or no spiritual or religious path. Focus on the outcome you desire and feelings burnable herbs give you and see how they affect you and your home's energy. The blends I create are designed for these purposes, to connect with the user and their intended outcomes, rather than the need to be historically or geographically connected to the ingredients.

Will you be creating it for any spiritual observances, or to contact specific Spirit Allies or deities you worship or work with? Find out what you think may resonate with these spirits and start there. Are these beings from certain world religions or mythologies? What part of the world would these beings and their devotees come from? For example, if Jesus is your patron deity, you may want to burn some frankincense and myrrh, or sandalwood to connect with Him, as these are classic and biblical resins that would have been used in those times, and based on stories that connect those resins to that deity. Are you a devotee of Odin or Thor? You may want to consider using mugwort, wormwood, cedar, juniper, sweetgrass, garden sage, chamomile or fennel, as some of these would be available to those in ancient and modern Scandinavia. What is sacred to Hekate? Diana? Cernunnos? You can see where I am going with this, just use your own judgement, and if you feel a being connects with an herb that you didn't expect and you really do feel that they like it, use it! The Gods are probably not as invested in specificities as we like to think, unless you have a deep devotion and really hear what they require from you. I do believe sometimes, they are happy to be recognized, especially the almost forgotten and very ancient ones. Our world is so small and so connected in these modern times, Gods and Goddesses are available to us all and call who they decide to call. The Gods aren't necessarily tied to the region of the world their ancient devotees were from, but also may appreciate the extra care in giving them things they are used to and are known to like.

Many magical practitioners create incense blends for spellwork and ritual with a specific amount of ingredients, day of the week and planetary correspondences, and association with the elements of earth, air, fire, or water. There are important reasons for these blends and the work the practitioner plans to do. I will not delve into these practices here, as there are books for the occult community that address this in far more depth than I can. I have created some of these for my own personal purposes, which will not be included in this book. I have not included on the plants lists any of these correspondences, as I have also found there to be some conflicting information, and will leave this up to you to decide what works.

Note: Be very careful if you delve deep into ancient uses for herbs in old books and grimoires. Many plants were used in magical and religious ritual offerings and are not suitable for burning. Some of these ingredients are unsustainable, not available, harmful, or poisonous. With modern science and information at our fingertips, we have knowledge of the natural world that would have been unheard of before. There are many books out there on magical associations of plants that are heavily based on old tomes and workings, with substitution lists for those plants that are now known to be toxic, not recommended to use, or no longer available. Do not be afraid to substitute one ingredient for another with similar properties. Be as safe as you can. Many modern herb books, such as Scott Cunningham's, have safe and sustainable substitutions. Do your homework and blend wisely!

Loose Incense Blend Recipes

Think about and infuse your blend with your intentions. If you want to take it farther, hold each herb in your dominant hand, place your energy into it, connect with it, think about the properties it has and why you are including it, and thank it as you put it into the blend. Grind into smaller bits if needed with a mortar and pestle, herb grinder, or your hands. Substitute with similar herbs or resins or change the ratios if needed. In witchcraft, many times we will choose the amount of ingredients for a recipe based on numerology. If this interests you. three, six, nine, and of course, lucky seven may resonate with you if you wish to put extra thought into your blend regarding that. If there is a number related to the work you are doing, add or subtract an ingredient from a blend. Be sure all plants are dried, not fresh. I have only included plants that I have written about here. I have also included little charms or mantras I wrote that you may use as you are holding and mixing these ingredients, if you wish, to make this an even more magical experience. Words have power, create and add to these if you wish. Make these blends your own!

Prosperity Blend

Success and wealth are mine to see, goodness and luck come to me.
I create joy abundantly, prosperity reigns supreme!

2 parts Palo Santo chips or powder
2 parts copal resin
1 part bay leaf
1 part mint
1 part chamomile
1 part juniper leaf or berry (or both)
1/2 part cinnamon chips

Body & Mind Purification Blend

Health is wealth, I am Well.
Body and mind in balance, I am Well.
My mind is clear, I am Well.
My heart is pure, I am Well.
I am whole and complete, I am Well.

1 part eucalyptus
1 part mullein
2 parts Yerba santa
2 parts white sage
1 part lavender buds
1 part frankincense resin

Heart Opening Blend

Love in my heart, love in my mind, love in my body, love is mine.

2 parts rose buds/petals
1 part lavender buds
1 part benzoin resin
1 part sweetgrass
1/2 part white sage

Spirit Ally Blend

Helper spirits heed my call, join me with love, friendship is all!*
Thank you allies, thank you friends, be with me now, on you I can depend.
(you can change Helper Spirits to the name of a specific spirit if needed)

1 part garden sage
1 part rosemary
2 parts mugwort
2 parts cedar
1 part frankincense resin

Soothing Sleep Blend

Sweet night, sweet dreams, my spirit take flight; my sleep is deep, I rest tonight!

1 part white sage
1 part lemon balm
1 part chamomile
2 parts mugwort
1 part benzoin resin

Purifying and Clarity Blend

Pure and clear, fresh and clean, my spirit is renewed, my vision keen.

2 parts palo Santo
1 part cedar/juniper
1 part Dragon's blood resin
1 part copal resin
1 part rosemary

Protection Blend

Blood of Dragon, wormwood, frankincense, and sandalwood.
Juniper, sage, and cinnamon, spice it up fiery and good.
Magic smoke, powerful, fine; protect us all, me and mine.

2 parts sandalwood
2 parts frankincense resin
1 part wormwood
1 part juniper berries
1 part garden sage
1 part Dragon's blood resin
1/2 part cinnamon chips

Endnotes

1. Rachel Patterson, *https://www.rachelpatterson.co.uk*
2. Emma J. Blain, Ahmed Y Ali, Victor Duance, *https://pubmed.ncbi.nlm.nih.gov/19943332/*
3. Chandra Shekhar Nautiyal, Puneet Singh Chauhan, Yeshwant Laxman Nene, *Medicinal Smokes, published 12/3/07 J Ethnopharmacol. 2007 Dec 3;114(3):446-51. Epub 2007 Aug 28. PMID:* 17913417
4. Migratory Bird Treaty Act 1918, *https://www.fws.gov/law/migratory-bird-treaty-act-1918*
5. The Chopra Center *https://chopra.com*
6. Heilung *https://heilung.bandcamp.com/music*
7. Hidden Hearth https://www.patreon.com/hiddenhearth
8. William S. Burroughs, *The Discipline of Do Easy*
9. Robin Artisson, *Upon The Rood Day: The Witchcraft of Christsonday and the Queen of Elphen*
10. Jason Miller, *Consorting With Spirits*
11. Jim Donovan, *https://www.donovanhealth.com*
12. Jonathan Goldman, *Vocal Toning The Chakras*
13. Alberto Villoldo, PhD, The Four Winds Society, *https://thefourwinds.com*

Bibliography

Alexander, Jane, *The Smudging and Blessing Book, Inspirational Rituals to Cleanse and Heal,* (Sterling, 2009)

Artisson, Robin, *Upon The Rood Day: The Witchcraft of Christonday and The Queen of Elphen Course* (Serpent Hall Institute, 2022)

Artisson, Robin, *Witching Way of the Hollow Hill, A Sourcebook of Hidden Wisdom, Folklore, Traditional Paganism, and Witchcraft,* (Pendraig, 2009)

Bradley, Kris, *Mrs. B's Guide to Household Witchery: Everyday Magic, Spells, and Recipes,* (Weiser, 2012)

Cunningham, Scott, *Encyclopedia of Magical Herbs,* (Llewellyn, 2012)

Cunningham, Scott, *Magical Herbalism, The Secret Craft Of The Wise,* (Llewellyn, 1985)

Cunningham, Scott, *The Complete Book of Incense, Oils, & Brews,* (Llewellyn, 2011)

Gladstar, Rosemary, *Medicinal Herbs, A Beginner's Guide,* (Storey, 2012)

Goldman, Jonathan, *Vocal Toning The Chakras,* CD (Sounds True, 2005)

McCampbell, Harvest, *Sacred Smoke, The Ancient Art of Smudging For Modern Times,* (Native Voices, 2002)

Miller, Jason, *Consorting With Spirits: Your Guide to Working with Invisible Allies,* (Weiser, 2022)

Miller, Richard Alan, *The Magical & Ritual Use of Herbs,* (Destiny, 1983)

Morris, Loren, *Braiding Magic, The Art of Crafting Spell Cords (forthcoming)*

Wachter, Aidan, *Six Ways: Approaches & Entries for Practical Magic,* (Ygret, Niche Publishing, 2018)

Wachter, Aidan, *Changeling: A Book Of Qualities,* (Ygret Niche Publishing, 2021)

Weiss and Weiss, *Growing and Using The Healing Herbs,* (Rodale, 1985)

Whitehurst, Tess, *The Good Energy Book, Creating Harmony and Balance For Yourself and Your Home,* (Llewellyn, 2012)

About the Author

Dawn Leith Dougherty lives in the rolling hills of rural North Carolina, USA, in the northern Piedmont region with her husband Ed "Greybeard", and SpookyKat, a tiny fuzzy black cat who somehow lost her tail. Together with her husband Ed, a woodworker and gifted flute maker, they are owners of Tree Of Life Designs, a true backyard enterprise and labor of love. They sell their wares on the internet, as well as at occasional music and craft festivals hither and yon.

Dawn is a Reiki Master – Teacher in the Usui System Of Natural Healing, an Ordained Priest in The Order Of Melchizedek, an Animist and Pagan, an early modern traditional Witch, a writer, a vocalist, musician, and performer in rock bands and stage productions, an amateur horticulturist, former florist, garden writer, and assistant manager of a garden center, and was once a featured zombie in a B horror movie. The love of plants, herbs, and pursuit of a magical life led her to seek energetic cleansing herbs and resins and study as much as possible about this compelling subject. Her and Ed love good incense, and as a result have developed their own brand of Tree Of Life Incense loose herbal blends.

Find Dawn on the web at www.treeoflifedesigns, and Facebook and Instagram at Tree Of Life Designs

Acknowledgements

I wish to bestow a hearty thank you to the following people, who have touched my life in positive ways, encouraged my creativity and allowed me to blossom, those from whom I have learned volumes about life, love, and healing, and those who have changed my life for the better in every way:

My loving husband, Ed "Greybeard", without whom this book would not exist. My son Malcolm, the most wonderful child I could have ever wished for. My mother and her twin, my favorite aunt, and my sister Kristin, who are rocks of grace, beauty, kindness, love, and support. My close friends and confidantes, who are true Soul Family, and are always there for me, without whom my light and joy would be greatly diminished, you all know who you are! My late father, Larry, who was an amazing Dad and supported and encouraged me, and did everything he could to give me what I needed to become the person I am today. I miss you, Dad, and know you would be proud of me. Last, but not least, my Spirit Allies, Ancestors, and familiar helper spirits, who watch me bumble my way through life and hopefully don't chuckle too hard at my expense.

I also wish to thank the inspiring artists, writers, musicians, magical folk, herbalists and natural people too numerous to mention, from whom I have learned so much, and who have given me much joy, healing, comfort, fun, light, and love. To everyone who purchased and enjoyed this book, I am grateful and wish you and yours a healthy, happy, and prosperous life for all your days!

Dawn Leith Dougherty

MOON BOOKS

PAGANISM & SHAMANISM

What is Paganism? A religion, a spirituality, an alternative belief system, nature worship? You can find support for all these definitions (and many more) in dictionaries, encyclopaedias, and text books of religion, but subscribe to any one and the truth will evade you. Above all Paganism is a creative pursuit, an encounter with reality, an exploration of meaning and an expression of the soul. Druids, Heathens, Wiccans and others, all contribute their insights and literary riches to the Pagan tradition. Moon Books invites you to begin or to deepen your own encounter, right here, right now.

If you have enjoyed this book, why not tell other readers by posting a review on your preferred book site.

Bestsellers from Moon Books

Keeping Her Keys
An Introduction to Hekate's Modern Witchcraft
Cyndi Brannen
Blending Hekate, witchcraft and personal development together to create a powerful new magickal perspective.
Paperback: 978-1-78904-075-3 ebook 978-1-78904-076-0

Journey to the Dark Goddess
How to Return to Your Soul
Jane Meredith
Discover the powerful secrets of the Dark Goddess and transform your depression, grief and pain into healing and integration.
Paperback: 978-1-84694-677-6 ebook: 978-1-78099-223-5

Shamanic Reiki
Expanded Ways of Working with Universal Life Force Energy
Llyn Roberts, Robert Levy
Shamanism and Reiki are each powerful ways of healing; together, their power multiplies. Shamanic Reiki introduces techniques to help healers and Reiki practitioners tap ancient healing wisdom.
Paperback: 978-1-84694-037-8 ebook: 978-1-84694-650-9

Southern Cunning
Folkloric Witchcraft in the American South
Aaron Oberon
Modern witchcraft with a Southern flair, this book is a journey through the folklore of the American South and a look at the power these stories hold for modern witches.
Paperback: 978-1-78904-196-5 ebook: 978-1-78904-197-2